LILIES

LILIES

Richard Bird

SHOOTING STAR PRESS

A QUANTUM BOOK

Published by Shooting Star Press, Inc.
230 Fifth Avenue, Suite 1212
New York, NY 10001
USA

ISBN 1-57335-490-2

This book was produced by
Quantum Books Ltd
6 Blundell Street
London N7 9BH

Printed in China by Leefung-Asco Printers Ltd

CONTENTS

INTRODUCTION

WHY LILIES?

Lilies have the power to stand out or catch the eye whether they are in the wild, in a border or in a bunch of cut flowers: they have a presence that is impossible to ignore. As a consequence non-gardeners as well as gardeners have had a fascination with lilies for centuries. The reasons for their attraction are hard to define; perhaps their charm lies in the fact that they have a simplicity and purity of form and colour and yet at the same time they are tinged with an exotic quality that exudes excitement. Certainly, exclamations are not unusual when they are seen in the garden or received in a bunch of flowers.

Not all gardeners grow lilies, as people are frequently under the misapprehension that they are difficult plants. However, more and more gardeners are getting caught under their spell, and once they are, it is very rare to find a garden with only one variety; once a gardener is hooked he or she will usually go on to grow many different varieties.

LEFT Flowers of the same strain can appear in many different colours. Shown is Harlequin Strain.
~

LEFT Bouquet of Alstromeria, 'Sunflight' (yellow lily) and 'Compass' (orange lily).
~

On the whole, lilies are hardy plants and do not present too much difficulty in cultivation. Pests and disease are the only real problems but even these, with good husbandry and careful use of modern chemicals, can easily be overcome. Lilies are not too greedy in terms of space, being happy to live between other plants with which they often blend very well. They associate particularly well with shrubs, the greenery of which acts as a wonderful foil to the blooms, and frequently fill gaps that other plants are shy to use.

LILIES IN CULTIVATION

Paintings on walls and on ceramics tell us that lilies have been popular for at least 35 centuries: the earliest illustrations we know of are those produced by the Minoan civilization on the Mediterranean island of Crete in the 15th century BC. The lilies depicted are *Lilium candidum*, whose popularity has been sustained to the present day. The Romans brought this lily with them across Europe to Britain where it became, in the Middle Ages, venerated as a sacred flower and associated with the Virgin Mary, thus acquiring its vernacular name of the Madonna lily. Towards the end of the 16th century it was supplemented by several of the other European species, in particular *L. martagon*, and by 1629 the first of the American lilies, *L. canadense*, the meadow lily, arrived in Europe from Canada.

By the 19th century, lilies were being introduced to Europe from the Far East, from China and Japan. Plant collecting had started in earnest during that century and continued into the 20th century, with new plants constantly being introduced. Surprisingly, one of the most popular of the lilies, *L. regale*, the regal lily, was not introduced into cultivation until 1903 when the well-known plant collector, EH Wilson, sent back bulbs from China.

All these introductions were species from the wild. It was not until the 19th century that the first European hybrids were seen. It is surprising since lilies have been in cultivation for so long that no hybrids had been produced earlier, although some were reputed

ABOVE: Lilium candidum *has been depicted since ancient times.*

~

to have been raised in Japan. A steady trickle of hybrids was created throughout the 19th century, increasing in number at the beginning of the 20th century. More interest was shown after the Second World War, and since then hundreds of hybrids have been created to satisfy the thirst of gardeners and lily fanciers throughout the world.

Lilies were not grown widely in North America until the end of the 19th century. By the early part of that century, native plants from the east coast, such as *Lilium superbum*, had been introduced into some gardens and four foreign lilies were being grown, including the ubiquitous *L. martagon*. By mid-century, plants were being introduced from the west coast and more foreign species were entering America. They were still relatively unusual in American gardens, compared with Europe, until towards the end of the century, when their popularity increased and their development in terms of new introductions and hybridization mirrored that in Europe.

ABOVE Lilium superbum, *an eastern American native, was introduced into gardens by the end of the 19th century.*
~

BELOW Lilium martagon *gained in popularity at the end of the 16th century.*
~

ABOVE Lilium regale *was introduced in 1903 by plant collector E H Wilson.*
~

Lilies are mainly plants of temperate areas of the world. They are found in all such regions in the northern hemisphere, from Siberia to India and from Europe to China and Japan, and also in North America. Depending on which classification you follow, there are about 80 species and innumerable subspecies scattered throughout this region, many of which have been grown by gardeners and, ultimately, have led to many hundreds of cultivated varieties.

There are one or two species, such as *Lilium martagon*, which are widely spread throughout the northern hemisphere, but the majority of them are confined to relatively small areas. Unlike many other plants with such a wide distribution, lilies are not common plants and in some cases a great deal of searching may be required to see them in the wild. This is particularly true of areas near habitation where lilies have often been collected out of existence.

While North America can boast quite a number of species there are none which are native to the British Isles. *Lilium martagon*, however, has become naturalized in a number of countries, including some areas of Britain, occasionally forming large colonies. *L. pyrenaicum* has also escaped from gardens in a few places.

The variety of habitat is extensive, varying from open mountainsides and grasslands to light woodland. Because of the predation of goats and other animals, lilies are often found, even in open countryside, hidden amongst bushes and scrub away from the grazing animals. They will tolerate quite moist conditions, sometimes being found in ditches or boggy areas; on the other hand they are not too keen on very dry areas.

THE STRUCTURE OF THE LILY

The lily is a bulbous plant that produces unbranched stems bearing from one to fifty flowers. The shape and size of the flowers vary considerably and are one of the criteria for their classification. Lilies are normally considered to be perennials but some are short-lived and need to be propagated regularly to keep them in cultivation.

THE FLOWERS

For most people, quite naturally, it is the flower which is the most important part of the lily. The actual shape of the flower and the way it is held varies considerably; these will be considered in a moment. First, it is important to look at the structure of the flower.

To the non-botanist a lily appears to have six petals, but, in fact, three of them are what are known technically as sepals. The difference between sepals and petals is that the sepals enclose the true petals when the flower is in bud; they form a protective sheath around the bud. In some species the sepals are narrower than the petals. The petals and sepals are collectively known as the perianth, and individually as perianth segments. (Alternatively, they are known by the shorter name of tepals.)

Lily flowers exist in a wide range of colours, blue being the one colour that is absent. Some flowers are of a single colour

LEFT Lilium longiflorum *has a trumpet-shaped flower.*
~

LEFT Nectary furrows are at the base of the perianth.
~

THE PARTS OF A LILY PLANT

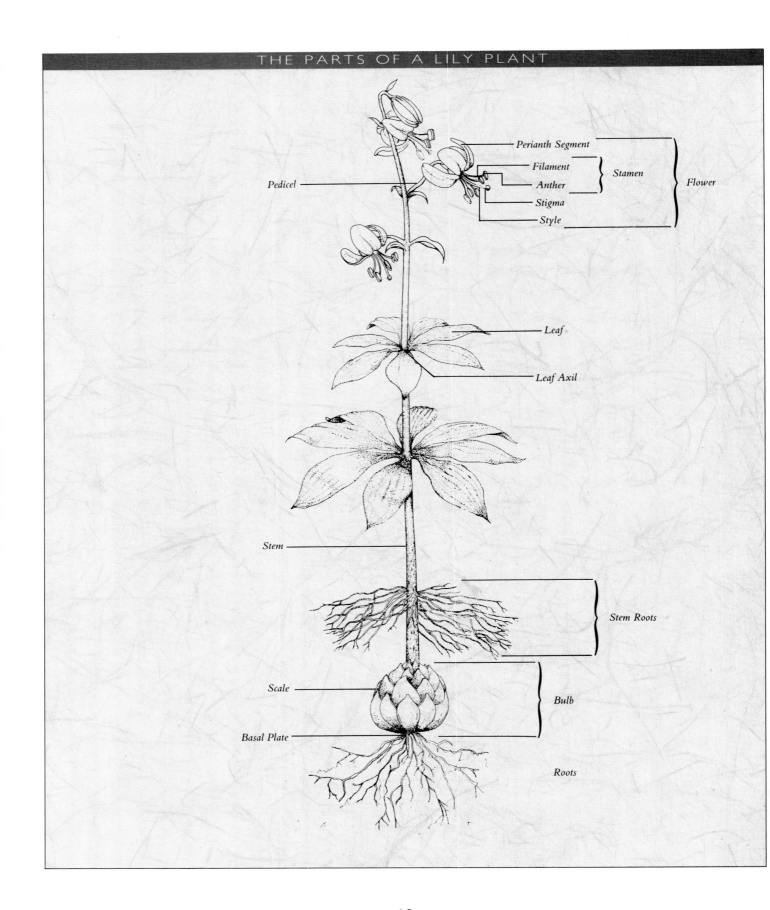

Pedicel

Perianth Segment

Filament

Anther

Stamen

Stigma

Style

Flower

Leaf

Leaf Axil

Stem

Stem Roots

Scale

Bulb

Basal Plate

Roots

ABOVE *The brightly coloured sexual parts – stamens and style – of*
Lilium speciosum rubrum.
~

while others are a mixture of colours and include stripes or spots. Some are subtle in their coloration while others are exceedingly brash.

At the base of each perianth segment is a nectary furrow, a groove in which nectar is produced as an enticement to insects to visit the plant and thus pollinate it.

The sexual parts that are associated with this pollination protrude from the centre of the flower. They consist of six stamens and a single style. On the stamens, the anthers are joined to the filament by their centres about which they are hinged. This allows maximum contact with a bee's body when it is collecting nectar from near the base of the stamens.

The colour of the anthers and the pollen varies from species to species and is a characteristic which helps in identification. I once had the embarrassing experience of walking around a famous garden unknowingly carrying pollen on the end of my nose until I met the head gardener, who, with a laugh, told me what lily I had been smelling. This pollen can also cause stains and it is often removed from lilies used as cut flowers to prevent it blemishing the table underneath.

The style is longer than the stamens and is surmounted by a three-lobed stigma, which is the sticky organ that receives the pollen. At the base of the style is the ovary, which on pollination of the stigma is fertilized and swells to form the seed capsule.

There is a great variation in the shape of different lily flowers. One of the most distinct is the Turk's cap shape in which the narrow petals and sepals are reflexed, that is turned back on themselves, so that the tips are almost touching above the flower,

forming a ball, while the stamens hang below. *Lilium martagon* is a prime example of this type.

Of a completely different form are the funnel-shaped flowers. These have overlapping perianth segments which form a tube, flaring outwards at its end. A well-known example of this is *L. candidum*. Closely allied to these are the trumpet-shaped lilies which have narrower and longer tubes. The difference between the two is only a matter of degree and many species and hybrids are referred to as being of either category. *L. longiflorum* is an example of the trumpet group.

Bowl-shaped lilies are another popular form. With these the broad segments gently flair outwards to form a bowl. In the star-shaped or cup-shaped flowers the segments arch very gradually and are not so recurved (or bent back) at the tips as the previous type. The last category is the bell-shaped lily in which the segments are straight and do not curve outwards; these flowers generally tend to be pendant, or hang downwards.

BELOW Lilium candidum *has a funnel-shaped flower.*
~

None of these categories are mutually exclusive and they are not official classes of lilies. They are simply broad categories which help with the description of the flowers.

As well as variation in shape there is also great diversity in the way the flowers are presented. The length of the flower stalk, the pedicel, varies, as does its angle with the main stem. Some lilies dangle the flowers delicately, others almost seem to thrust them towards the viewer, while others hold them up to the heavens.

THE SEED

Lilium martagon album

Lilium pumilum

Lilium henryi

Once the flower has been pollinated and the segments begin to wither, the ovary swells as the seeds develop. These seeds vary in size, but are usually big enough to be handled individually. Lily seeds often appear rather two-dimensional in that they are a raised lump surrounded by a light brown, papery wing.

The seeds are stacked inside a capsule one on top of the other in three sections. The capsule, which can vary in shape in different lilies, is held upright and splits from the top forming a chalice-shaped container in which the seeds repose until some movement disturbs them. Lily seeds must be one of the easiest for the gardener to collect since, unless there is a strong wind, they will remain in position for several, if not many, days.

The papery membrane around the seed acts as a crude wing which carries the seed on the wind away from the parent plant. The weight of the seed is great relative to the surface area and aerodynamic properties of the wing, and so seeds do not usually travel far; just sufficient to start a new colony some distance away from the parent.

The seed pods have their own beauty and add structure and interest to the border long after the flower has passed away. They are also very useful in dried-flower arrangements, especially the giant pods of *Cardiocrinum giganteum*, a lily relative.

THE STEMS

On the other side of the basal plate, within the bulb, is the growing point which expands into the stem. The growing point is often visible when bulbs are purchased and care should be taken not to damage it.

As the growing season progresses, this point elongates into a single stem up to 10 ft (3 m) tall. It is only when it reaches flowering height that the stem may divide. It is important to remember this because, if either the growing point or the stem is damaged, growth is halted and no new growth will be produced that year.

In many lilies, the part of the stem below ground forms stem roots. These radiate outwards, with the dual functions of helping to anchor the plant and collecting nutrients from the humus-rich top layer of the soil. The strength of the stem plus the abundance of anchoring roots means that most lilies require little staking unless exposed to strong winds.

Another feature of the below-ground portion of the stem in many of the species is the production of the bulblets. As the flower stem dies back, so the bulblets are left to grow on. These are a ready means of propagating lilies. In some species other small bulbs, bulbils, are formed above ground in the axils (between the leaves and the stems). Again, as the stem dies the bulbils form roots, this time falling to the ground ready to enter the soil. These bulbils can be collected by the gardener and 'sown'.

As has already been seen, not all stems rise directly from the bulb. In the stoloniform group the stem can wander some distance, sometimes up to 20 in (50 cm), before it surfaces.

ABOVE Bulbils form along the stem of some lilies.
~

ABOVE *The bulb of an Asiatic hybrid lily.*
~

ABOVE *The bulb of an Oriental hybrid lily.*
~

The lily bulb is distinct in that it is made up of many scales which overlap, somewhat resembling the unopened flower-head of a globe artichoke. These scales are quite visible since they do not possess a papery covering, or tunic, as do most other bulbs. The main function of these scales is to act as food storage organs and, as we will see later, they can be used to propagate further lilies.

Other features of the bulb are the basal plate (which, as its name suggests, is formed underneath the bulb), the roots (which descend from the basal plate), and the growing point (which produces the stem and which forms on the top of the basal plate).

There are five different types of lily bulb. The commonest form, to which the bulk of lilies belong, are concentric bulbs. These are

roughly circular with the growing point in or near the middle, surrounded by the scales; *L. candidum, L. martagon* and *L. regale* are common examples. Rhizomatous bulbs form connected mats of bulbs where the bulb branches, producing two or more growing points surrounded by scales. The leopard lily, *L. pardalinum*, is a good example of this type. In between the two are the sub-rhizomatous bulbs, which extend in one direction only. *L. columbianum, L. humboldtii* and *L. washingtonianum* are typical of this form. The fourth type are the stoloniferous bulbs. Here the bulbs send out stolons below ground, at the tip of which new bulbs are formed. *L. canadense* and *L. superbum* are familiar examples of this type of bulb. The final group are the stoloniform bulbs. These again send out horizontal stolons but this time the new bulbs are formed along their length and the tip turns up forming the flowering stem.

The roots emerge from beneath the basal plate, mainly around its perimeter. There are two types of root: feeder and contractile. The former, as its name suggests, are concerned with supplying the plant with its food and water. These roots can easily be distinguished as they are smaller and more delicate than the contractile roots. The latter type form a much-branched network and pull the young bulb down to its correct depth in the soil. They are usually much thicker and stronger than the feeder roots. The contractile roots also help to keep tall plants steady in the ground. As will be seen later, some lilies form roots on their stems.

ABOVE *A* Lilium superbum *bulb.*
~

ABOVE *Lily growing fields in Oregon, USA.*
~

THE LEAVES

The leaves are either scattered up the stem or arranged at regular intervals in whorls. They vary in outline from strap-like to broad ovals. With a few exceptions they are sessile, that is stalkless. In some species bulbils grow in the junctions between the leaves and the stem as has already been described in the previous section. On the whole, the leaves are glabrous, or hairless, often with a fresh glossy look which enhances the appearance of the plant.

HORTICULTURAL CLASSIFICATION

If the gardener is simply growing lilies for the pleasure of having them in the garden then their classification is of little importance. On the other hand, if the bug really gets a hold and the gardener decides to put his or her blooms in for competition at flower shows then classification begins to take on an importance. Because of the great diversity in the shape and colour of the flowers it would be impossible to say that one was better than another, but by splitting them up into groups the judges are comparing like with like and the task becomes much easier.

ABOVE Lilies growing in fields, some of which will eventually be used in formal arrangements (RIGHT).

~

The classification that is generally accepted is the one drawn up by the Royal Horticultural Society of Britain, which is the international registering authority for lilies. In order to establish to which group a particular lily belongs, reference can be made to the *International Lily Register*, which lists the majority of hybrids, cultivars and strains in existence. The *Register* is maintained by the Royal Horticultural Society which issues annual supplements of new names. All serious lily growers should acquire the register plus its supplements, which now lists over 4,000 lilies. The classification below is taken from the 1982 edition.

Division I   Hybrids derived from such species or hybrid groups as *Lilium lancifolium* (*L. tigrinum*), *L. cernuum*, *L. davidii*, *L. leichtlinii*, *L. × maculatum*, *L. × hollandicum*, *L. amabile*, *L. pumilum*, *L. concolor* and *L. bulbiferum*.

I (a)   Early-flowering lilies with upright flowers, single or in an umbel.

I (b)   Those with outward-facing flowers.

I (c)   Those with pendant flowers.

Division II   Hybrids of martagon type of which one parent has been a form of *L. martagon* or *L. hansonii*.

Division III   Hybrids derived from *L. candidum*, *L. chalcedonicum*, and other related European species (but excluding *L. martagon*).

Division IV   Hybrids of American species.

Division V   Hybrids derived from *L. longiflorum* and *L. formosanum*.

Division VI   Hybrid trumpet lilies and Aurelian Hybrids derived from Asiatic species including *L. henryi*, but excluding those derived from *L. auratum*, *L. speciosum*, *L. japonicum* and *L. rubellum*.

VI (a)   Those with trumpet-shaped flowers.

VI (b)   Those with bowl-shaped and outward-facing flowers.

VI (c)   Those with pendant flowers.

VI (d)   Those with flat, star-shaped flowers.

Division VII   Hybrids of Far Eastern species such as *L. auratum*, *L. speciosum*, *L. japonicum* and *L. rubellum*, including any hybrids of *L. henryi*.

VII (a)   Those with trumpet-shaped flowers.

VII (b)   Those with bowl-shaped flowers.

VII (c)   Those with flat flowers.

VII (d)   Those with recurved flowers.

Division VIII   All hybrids not provided for in any other division.

Division IX   All species and their varieties and forms.

CULTIVATING LILIES

ACQUIRING PLANTS

ilies can be obtained in three ways: as bulbs, seed or bulbils, but most gardeners acquire their first plants as bulbs, usually from their local garden centre or nursery. Unless it is a big nursery the stock is likely to be restricted to a few cultivars, but this is normally sufficient to get the gardener hooked on growing them. To find a wider selection the grower must turn to the specialist firms who may have hundreds of both species and cultivars on offer.

Whether you buy from a general supplier or a specialist only ever buy sound bulbs. They can very easily be dried out or damaged in transit between the grower and the seller; both fates are likely to kill the plant. Injury to roots or scales can let in fungal infections, and any damaged or bruised parts should be removed and the remaining bulb treated with a fungicide to prevent further harm.

Never buy bulbs that have been desiccated, so avoid those that have been packed loose or have obviously been allowed to dry out in their peat or wood-shavings packaging. The best bulbs are those that have only recently been dug up from their nursery beds: these look moist and plump. Specialist suppliers are more likely to provide this type of bulb than the general garden centres

LEFT *Lilies are attractive in a perennial border, shown here highlighted with bright yellow evening primrose* (Oenothera sp.).
~

LEFT *A selection of healthy lily bulbs.*
~

ABOVE An informal planting of lilies and giant allium, with a flowering plum providing an attractive deep-coloured background.
~

which rely on buying in their bulbs, often through an intermediary, all of which takes time and its toll.

Once the gardener is set on the lily trail he or she will undoubtedly meet other similar enthusiasts and these can become a good source of material through gifts and exchanges of bulbs. The same conditions still prevail; only accept disease-free, undamaged plants.

On receipt of bulbs check that they are sound and treat with fungicide if necessary. If the bulbs are weak, plant them in a moist humus-rich soil placing them in a cool glasshouse for a couple of weeks until they have revived – the bulbs will look fresher and more alive. They are then ready to plant out assuming that the weather and soil conditions are right.

One way that bulbs should *not* be acquired, it must be heavily stressed, is from the wild. Wild stocks are being depleted by a wide range of causes, plant collectors being one of them, although development and pollution are often greater offenders. Leave the plants where they are, not only for others to appreciate, but to

keep a reservoir of pure stock in the wild that has not been contaminated either by crossing or by diseases in the garden.

Many growers are reluctant to allow any lily bulbs to enter their garden gates; they are too worried about virus and other diseases, and therefore propagate all their new plants from seed. To the beginner this may seem a slow and cumbersome method, but it does provide disease-free stock. If a few seeds are sown every year, the grower soon has a new selection of flowering plants. As well as helping to keep disease at bay, seed has other advantages – it is cheap and several bulbs of the same plant can be raised at once. It allows the gardener to acquire a greater range of material and certainly more of the species than would otherwise be possible.

There are a wide range of sources of seed. Friends may provide it, while general or specialized gardening societies are likely to run seed exchanges. Seed is often collected from the wild and offered for sale. (This is permissible as long as only 20% (10% for rarer species) of the seed is collected.) Seed can also, of course, be purchased from some of the more specialized seed merchants. Details of how to deal with seed once it has been acquired are given in the chapter on propagation.

Bulbils, which are produced on the stems of some of the species and cultivars of mature lilies, are similar to seed in that it is a while before mature plants become available. Bulbils, again like seeds, must be obtained fresh (although they will tolerate some drying out) and in a sound condition. They are normally acquired from fellow gardeners as there are few commercial sources. Their propagation will also be dealt with later.

CHOOSING THE SITE

Having acquired bulbs, or having propagated them, the gardener then needs to plant them out. The first thing is to choose the site. Most lilies like a sunny position although some are strict woodlanders and need shade. (The A–Z sections later in this book show which these are.) Although most enjoy the sun they do like their roots to be cool and this can best be achieved by growing them with other vegetation which shades the lower part of the plant, for example in a herbaceous or mixed border or amongst shrubs.

Lilies mix in well with other plants and are particularly at home amongst green-leaved shrubs as these will often make a backdrop against which the lilies are shown off to their best advantage. The lilies are likely to be flowering long after the shrubs have had their show of flowers and so add colourful interest to what could become a dull border. However, make sure that the shrubs are not too vigorous or close together so that they do not overshadow the lily: it is only the lower part of the stem that needs the shade.

For those people who are lucky enough to have larger gardens, many of the lily species do well in a wild setting of grass or light woodland, as long as the competition is not too severe or the shade too dense. Once established, the lilies will sow themselves around, building up quite large colonies. Martagon lilies, *L. martagon*, are prime candidates for this treatment.

In a more formal setting, lilies also mix in well in a herbaceous border. Here the selection of site must be more carefully chosen so that the colours are sympathetic and so that the lilies harmonize with the surrounding plants as the border is likely to be at its peak when the lilies are in bloom. The shapes and colours of the lilies make them exciting plants and they do much to enliven a border with their exotic presence. Even before flowering height

ABOVE Lilies planted at the edge of a meadow.

~

is reached the growing lily stems contribute to the texture of the border and act as a foil to other plants.

Do not mix lilies but keep to the same species or cultivar in each clump, otherwise the effect becomes too 'busy'; it will be restless to the eye. Try to plant in odd numbers, which somehow always look more natural and satisfying than even numbers.

It can be tempting to create a lily border, with nothing in it except lilies. This should be avoided. Lilies look better mixed with other plants, and, more importantly, disease can pass through a monoculture of lilies like wildfire. Lilies separated by other plants in a herbaceous border or shrubbery are more protected. Aphids carrying a deadly virus, for example, are less likely to move from one lily to another, as the intervening plants will act as physical barriers.

PREPARING THE SOIL

Lilies like the classic conditions of a free-draining, moisture-retentive soil. In spite of appearance, these two conditions do not cancel each other out. Free-draining means that any excessive water can easily drain away, leaving sufficient moisture, usually held in humus, to supply the plant.

Wet, stagnant conditions will cause the bulbs to rot. If the soil is inclined to be wet, some form of drainage system should be installed. Alternatively a deep raised bed could be built, containing a better soil, so that the bulbs are lifted above the surrounding area. Heavy soil should be lightened with the addition of grit and humus, the latter in the form of manure or compost, both of which should be well-rotted.

A dry soil should have organic material added to it. This not only provides the plants with moisture held in its fibrous texture, but also supplies nutrients which are likely to have been leached away in the rapidly drained soil.

The soil should have a good depth to it and should be prepared to at least 20 in (50 cm). Double digging with humus, and grit if necessary, added to the lower as well as the upper spit is the best way of achieving this. Prepare a decent-sized area and ensure that any water that collects in the bottom of the bed can drain away, as small areas thus prepared can act as sumps and partially fill with water with dire consequences to the lilies.

If well-rotted manure or compost has been added to the soil as it is dug then no further fertilizers need adding at the time of preparation. If manure or compost has not been added, then a general fertilizer with a balanced formula can be added and well raked in. Later, as we will see, the ground can be top-dressed with a potash-rich fertilizer.

The acidity of the soil should be about neutral, pH 7. This can be tested with a simple kit for pH testing available at garden centres and nurseries. For some lilies it will be necessary to adjust the soil pH with lime to raise the alkalinity. Other soils may possibly need humus added, which tends to make soil more acid, but pH 7 will suit most lilies and there should be little need to alter it.

A very important point to note is that when the soil is prepared all perennial weeds should be eliminated, through hard weeding or perhaps with the aid of chemical herbicides. Once the lilies are in place it is essential that they are not disturbed as they are brittle. Any attempts to remove perennial weeds at this stage could cause damage that will not be repaired until the next season. Annual weeds are not so important as most of them are surface-rooting, but they still use up moisture and nutrients as well as harbouring disease.

OPPOSITE *Lilies can be colour-coordinated in a garden as in this pink garden with* Lilium speciosum rubrum, *hollyhock* (Alcea sp.) *and bee balm* (Monarda didyma), *or they can be contrasted with delphinium and calendulas, for example (* ABOVE *).*
~

PLANTING

Once the site has been chosen and the ground prepared then the bulbs can be planted. This can be done at any time as long as the ground is not frozen, with the optimum time being in the spring, once there is sufficient warmth for growth to take place.

Most lilies should be deeply planted, especially those that have stem roots which appear above the bulb. As a rule of thumb, a bulb should planted so that its tip is below the ground at a depth equivalent to twice or two and a half times the height of the bulb. It does not matter if the bulb is planted a little too shallow, as the contractile roots will adjust it downwards if necessary.

There are a few lily bulbs, notably those of *Lilium candidum* and *Cardiocrinum giganteum*, which need a shallow planting, with their tips just below the surface. If a shallow planting depth is necessary for a particular plant it will be pointed out in the A–Z sections later in the book.

Fortunately lily bulbs leave you in no doubt as to which is top and which is bottom so there should be no problem in planting them the right way up, with the growing point at the top and the basal plate and roots at the bottom.

Many growers put a layer of grit or sharp sand into the hole before planting the lily directly on top of it. The reason for this is twofold. In the first instance the grit prevents the bulb from lying on damp soil, as it drains the water away, and secondly the grit is said to help keep slugs at bay.

The soil around the bulb should be moist at the time of planting and the bulbs should be watered in if necessary.

A mulch of chipped bark or well-rotted compost can be applied with benefit after the bulb has been planted. This not only helps keep the weeds down and conserves moisture, but also helps keep the root run cool.

SUBSEQUENT ATTENTION

If a mulch of bark or compost has been applied then this considerably reduces the amount of subsequent attention that the bulbs require. If the mulch is thick enough (4 in/10 cm is a good depth), it will help keep down annual weeds and will reduce the amount of watering necessary in dry spells.

Mulching with farmyard manure can be very beneficial to those lilies that are left in the ground for a number of years. It adds extra nutrients, and worms will work the humus down into the soil, conditioning it and helping to conserve moisture. Manure should be well-rotted and not fresh, as fresh manure can harm the growing lily. Farmyard manure that is not well-rotted and garden compost may contain seeds which then produce weeds which are often difficult to eradicate. Therefore, a top dressing of manure covered with bark is an excellent precaution.

If roots are seen appearing from the lower part of the lily's stem then these need covering with either a mulch or soil.

When plants are top-dressed with manure once a year they may only need the occasional liquid feed to top up their strength during the growing season. Otherwise a granular feed can be applied in the spring. This should be a balanced fertilizer with equal proportions of nitrogen (N), phosphorus (P) and potassium (K) in its make-up. (A fertilizer's make-up is indicated by the NPK formula on the label, 7–7–7 having equal proportions of each element whereas 5–6–10 has proportionately higher quantities of phosphorus and potassium than nitrogen.) Liquid feed can also be given during the growing season. This can have a lower nitrogen and a higher potassium content; tomato fertilizer (7–7–10), for example, being a good feed to use. Wood ash makes a good addition to the soil as this is quite high in potash (potassium) and can be applied as a top-dressing.

Lilies prefer not to get too dry and should be watered in dry weather. Make certain that the watering is thorough and does not just dampen the top half-inch of the soil. The water must penetrate to the roots to do any good. In dry areas where rain is not to be expected, a permanent watering system can be installed.

The majority of lilies are strong enough to stand up by themselves, but since some of the cultivars have large heavy flowers they may need support. Others may also need support in exposed areas where strong winds can do a lot of damage. A simple system can be adopted using canes to which the lily stems are tied. Another possibility where there is a clump to be supported is to insert some pea sticks into the ground around the clump, bending over their tops and interlacing them to form a network of twigs through which the lilies will grow. In either case be careful not to spear the bulbs when inserting the cane or stick. It can be advantageous to mark the positions of the bulbs when planting, or even insert the stakes at this time if you do not mind their presence, so that the danger of 'spearing' both bulbs and roots may be avoided.

OPPOSITE *Lilies ('Enchantment') look well when backed by evergreen shrubs.*

BELOW *A mulch helps to keep weeds under control while keeping the lily bulbs cool; here the lilies are mulched with grass clippings.*
~

Once the flowers are over, the head should be removed to prevent the bulb wasting any energy on seed production – the flower-heads should be retained, of course, if seed is required. The deadheading should take place just beneath the flower-head, leaving the remainder of the stem plus its leaves. These will then be able to continue photosynthesizing and producing food which will allow the bulb to rebuild its reserves for the following season. The dead or dying stem can be removed in autumn.

Most lilies are fairly hardy, but in cold areas it might be necessary to top up the mulching over the bulbs as added protection against excessive frosts. Mulch can harbour slugs which are one of the lily's worst enemies during its winter dormancy, so try to reduce their populations or apply slug pellets.

REPLANTING

Lilies, like most plants, need replanting every so often, usually because they have multiplied to such an extent that they have become congested, or perhaps because they would look better in another position. The best time to replant is just after the lilies have finished flowering, while they are still able to put out new growth. They will undoubtedly flag, particularly in hot weather. If a long period of hot weather is expected it may be better to delay the operation until the autumn, when it is likely to be cooler. There is no real disadvantage to replanting at this later time except that there is not so much growing time left in the year for the plants to re-establish themselves.

The soil for replanted bulbs should be prepared in the same way as described above for newly planted bulbs. It is during replanting that light soils come into their own as it is possible to move the bulbs without doing too much damage to the roots or to the bulb itself. Every care must be taken to ensure that the roots and bulb are not damaged, not only to give the lily a good chance of resuming their growth, but because injury can cause rotting and death.

LILIES IN CONTAINERS

It is not necessary to grow lilies in the open ground; they can be grown equally well in containers, or, as we shall see in the next section, under glass. The big advantage of containers is that they can be positioned anywhere, including places that would otherwise be unsuitable for plants, such as paved terraces or patios. Another advantage is that the gardener is in full control of the soil that is used. This means that acid-loving lilies, such as *L. auratum*, can be grown in a lime-free soil mix in a garden that

ABOVE Many lilies can be grown successfully in containers, providing they are well fed and well watered.
~

has a chalky soil. If the pots are not too heavy they can be moved about, even indoors if so desired.

Any container can be used as long as it is deep enough to contain the bulb and its roots. This means the container should preferably be able to hold at least 1 ft (30 cm) depth of soil. It must also have enough holes in the bottom to allow free and unimpeded drainage. Try to choose something that is in keeping with the dignity of the plant: stone or terracotta containers are generally more sympathetic than plastic. The latter do have the advantage of not drying out so rapidly but can become waterlogged in excessively wet weather.

Before filling the container and planting it up, place it in its final position – a large pot full of soil weighs a great deal and accidents can so easily happen when such pots are being moved.

The bottom of the containers should be 'crocked', ie the drainage holes should be covered with pieces of tile or pebbles so that, while drainage is unimpeded, the soil will not be washed out through the holes. A layer of small stones or gravel will further aid drainage. On top of this put a potting mixture: the mixture should be a third each by volume of good garden loam, grit and well-rotted compost, preferably of leaves. Depending on the amount of sand or grit already in the loam it may be necessary to add a bit extra to ensure that drainage is adequate. To this a small quantity of a general fertilizer can be added.

The bulbs should be planted at the same depth as they would be in the open garden. They can be planted in autumn or in the spring. Autumn-planted ones may need moving under cover or otherwise given winter protection from frosts as these can freeze the soil solid.

The problem with all container-grown plants is that they need constant attention with regard to watering, and feeding as well. They must not be allowed to dry out, nor must they be over-watered so that the bulbs rot. Nutrients are quickly leached from the soil in containers, washed out by the water draining through and out of the base. Consequently, container-grown lilies will need a liquid feed added to the water at least once a fortnight. This, again, can be a tomato feed.

The soil in the pots will become exhausted very quickly and will need replacing every year. The bulbs should be repotted in the autumn. This is a simple process following the pattern outlined above.

LILIES UNDER GLASS

The big advantage of a glasshouse is that the gardener can control the environment; lilies can be provided with warmth and moisture at the gardener's, and not the weather's, command. This means that plants usually start into growth earlier than they would outside and consequently the flowering season can be extended by raising early blooms inside. A glasshouse also lets the gardener attend to the plants at a convenient time, rather than be held up because the soil is too wet or frozen during the only time he or she has free. As with containers, the grower is able to control more accurately the medium in which the lilies are growing. A final advantage, and to many growers a very important one, is that lilies that are too tender to be risked outside can be grown.

Growing lilies under glass seems the ideal but there are problems. They need much more attention both with regard to watering and feeding. The worst problem is that pests and diseases also appreciate the ideal indoor conditions and become more difficult to control. Other pests and diseases that are not experienced outside may also occur.

Another problem is that it is quite expensive to heat a glasshouse. Heating bills, plus the additional costs of composts and so on, can make glasshouse cultivation an expensive operation. However, having said this, gardeners should not be discouraged from this approach if it appeals to them and their pocket will stretch to it.

ABOVE Lilies in a perennial border with campanula and helianthus.
~

The simplest way to grow lilies in glasshouses is in containers, as already described, but with the advantage of being able to control the atmospheric conditions. In winter, the temperature can be kept just above freezing, or, if earlier flowering is required, it can be stepped up to a minimum of about 45°F (8°C). During the summer the problem is keeping the glasshouse cool. As much ventilation as possible should be given and shading should be applied either in the form of netting or slats, or by applying a shading compound or white-wash to the outside of the glass. Evaporation of water sprayed onto the central path will also help to keep the house cool. Unless the pots are too heavy or there is nowhere to put them, many can be moved out into the open during the summer, which will give the plants a more natural atmosphere. Do not put the plants out if heavy rainstorms are expected.

Lilies under glass need not be confined to pots. It is possible, and indeed preferable in some cases, to grow them in a specially prepared bed in the glasshouse. Stoloniferous lilies, which 'wander' through the soil, prefer this. The bed can be excavated from the floor of the house or built up from it in the form of a raised bed. The soil used should be the same as used in containers and the treatment will be essentially the same. With a bigger volume of soil, the bed should not dry out so quickly.

Whether the bulbs are in containers or in beds they can be planted in autumn or mid winter and then treat as for container plants grown outside. Particular attention must be paid to any pest or disease that invades the glasshouse (these will be dealt with in a later chapter), as once present pests and diseases can build up to devastating proportions in a very short time.

PROPAGATION

T here can be few gardeners who do not get great satisfaction from propagating their own plants. In an active garden propagation becomes an essential part of the annual routine as it is not only a question of raising new plants but also a way to ensure the continuing survival of some of the rarer or more difficult occupants of the borders and beds. Propagation also helps ensure the survival of plants in the wild; if bulbs are propagated in cultivation then there is less need for anybody to dig up those from the countryside and of course, the less depredation of these wild stocks the better. To the lily grower, propagation means all these things and more besides.

SEED

One of the most fundamental ways of propagating plants is through the germination of seed. To lily growers seed germination has several advantages. It allows them to propagate lilies that are difficult to obtain as bulbs; it allows them to produce cheaply more bulbs of the same plant than they could afford to buy if purchased as mature bulbs; and it allows them to raise their own hybrid stock.

However, the most valid reason for raising plants from seed is that bulbs so raised are free of virus infections that can be so easily introduced with purchased material. Once these diseases have been introduced they are difficult to eradicate and can quickly run through the whole stock, distorting or killing all the lily bulbs in the garden. Seed-produced bulbs are virus-free even if the seed comes from plants that are themselves infected.

Before describing the techniques, there should be a warning about the limitations of growing from seed. If the seed comes from a species, particularly one in the wild, where there has been no hybridization then there is a good chance that the ensuing plant will resemble the parent. However, seed from cultivars, hybrids or species that have crossed with nearby plants will not necessarily produce offspring that are identical to their parents, in fact the chances are they will not. Any plants raised from seed of a cultivar must not be given the same name as the parent. (Vegetatively propagated bulbs will be a true replica of their parent and can bear the same name, as we will see later in this chapter.)

Lily seeds make life complicated by having two different methods of germination, epigeal or hypogeal. Lilies belong to

LEFT The sexual parts of a flower, so important for hybridization, are clearly visible in this bloom of Lilium 'Discovery'.
~

the monocotyledons, ie they only produce one seed leaf, the first leaf to emerge from the seed. In epigeal germination this cotyledon emerges in the conventional manner above ground, carrying the seed case on its tip or losing it as it passes up through the soil. With hypogeal germination the cotyledon and seed case remain out of sight, below ground near the developing bulb, and the first leaf to be seen above the surface is the first true leaf.

Further complications set in as the germination can be either immediate or delayed. Immediate germination, as its name implies, means that as soon as the seed meets favourable conditions it will start into growth and continue like any other germinating seed. With delayed germination, it may be up to two or more years before the seed germinates or appears to germinate. In fact, in many cases the seed may start germinating, but then stop until the return of favourable conditions. Delayed germination is mainly a hypogeal phenomenon. Germination will commence unseen below ground and then halt until the following spring when the first true leaf will appear above ground. This is obviously an adaptation to ensure survival in the climatic conditions that the bulb expects to meet in the wild. Immediate response tends to relate more to epigeal germination, but there are exceptions to both situations.

Epigeal/hypogeal and immediate/delayed germinations are interesting side-glances into the physiology of lilies but what do they mean in practical terms? Well, with regard to immediate/delayed germination the obvious first point must be made that pots of ungerminated lily seed should not be thrown away for at least three years after sowing as there is still the possibility that plants will emerge. The second is that immediate epigeal seed can be sown in spring when the conditions required for germination are present, namely, moisture, warmth and light, although many growers sow the seed fresh in the autumn; delayed hypogeal seed should, if possible, be sown in autumn when conditions are right for germination. They will then stop developing during the cold winter, and begin growing again in the warmer spring. If sowing is delayed until the spring there will be no cold spell until the following winter and germination will not occur until the following spring.

Seed should be sown in pots containing a free-draining soil mixture. Pots are preferable as the modern plastic trays are too shallow. The soil should be a gritty seed mix or one low in fertilizer specially formulated for sowing seed. A loam-based mixture should be used if the young bulbs are to be left in the pot until their second year, as humus-rich seed mixtures will not have enough nutrients to sustain growth for this length of time. If a loam-based mixture is used it should have extra grit or

horticultural sand added to aid drainage. A home-made soil mixture should contain a third each by volume of loam, grit and well-composted leaves. A small quantity (as directed on the packet) of base fertilizer can be added to the mixture to bring it up to the strength for plants that are to be left in the pot.

Sow the seed *thinly* over the top of the soil, placing each seed individually if necessary to ensure even distribution. Some growers prefer to stand the seed on its edge. Cover the seeds with a layer of grit and then water, either from above with a watering can or from below by standing the pots in a tray of water until the soil is moist. The pots should be placed in a shaded spot either in the open, or in an open cold frame. There is no need to protect them except from excessive rain. Outside the pots will experience winter frosts which will help the delayed germinating seed produce leaves in the spring. Keep the pots moist and water regularly once germination has taken place; you should aim to keep the young bulbs in leaf for as long as possible. Weak liquid feed, low in nitrogen and high in potassium, can be applied with the water every two weeks or so.

It is essential to label the pots as the seed is sown. Most gardeners at some time or other have fallen into the trap of thinking that they will remember what is in a particular pot only to forget completely. The label should contain the full name of the plant, the source of the seed and the date of sowing. If the grower is experimenting with different mixtures then the one used should also be recorded. It may be worthwhile to note the same information in a book to provide a more permanent record of plants the gardener grows or propagates. The point may seem trivial or uninteresting to beginners, but the accumulation of data will eventually provide a mine of information and greatly help to increase the grower's knowledge.

Most growers prefer to transplant the young seedlings at the end of their first summer, either into pots or into specially enriched ground. The operation is a delicate one because the young plants can so easily be damaged. One possible way of avoiding the damage is to sow the seed in individual pots, and then plant the whole pot out, or pot it on to a larger container, without disturbing the roots. With slower-growing subjects some growers prefer to leave young bulbs in the pots until the end of their second year to allow them to get the maximum undisturbed growth before they are potted up individually.

Delayed hypogeal seed that is obtained too late to plant in the autumn can be sown and kept in a warm place until the seedlings have been formed. They should then be transferred to a domestic refrigerator for three months to chill, before placing them in a frame and continuing as normal. This speeds up the whole process.

PROPAGATION USING SEEDS

1. A POT WITH FREE-DRAINING SOIL IS PERFECT FOR PLANTING LILY SEEDS.

2. SOW THE SEED THINLY OVER THE SOIL.

3. COVER THE SEED WITH A LAYER OF SOIL.

4. *LILIUM CENTIFOLIUM* 2 MONTHS AFTER SOWING SEED.

Instead of using pots the seed can be added to a mixture of humus-rich soil and grit in a polythene bag. The mixture should be just moist. The same procedure is followed as described above except that when the bag comes out of the refrigerator the seedlings need to be potted up. Careful handling is required as the seedlings can easily be damaged.

With some species it is possible to sow the seeds directly into drills in the soil as one would with most vegetables. If sown thinly the plants can be left undisturbed until the bulbs have fully developed. In colder or wetter districts the same effect can be achieved by direct sowing in soil in a cold frame.

SCALING

If the gardener wants to produce bulbs that retain the same characteristics as the parent then propagation must be undertaken vegetatively, in other words by inducing part of the parent bulb to reproduce itself. There are several methods of doing this but one of the most popular, and a method almost unique to lilies, is by using scales.

Depending on how many bulbs are wanted, just one or two scales can be removed or the whole bulb can be descaled. Only healthy bulbs should be used and the required number of scales should be cleanly snapped off as close to the base as possible. The wounded area on both the bulb and the scale should be dusted with a fungicide. If only a few scales have been removed then the bulb can be replanted. It is even possible to take just one or two scales from the side of a bulb without removing it from the ground; simply remove the soil on one side, snap off the required scales and replace the soil after dusting the wounds with fungicide.

The scales can be taken at any time of the year and different growers have different preferences. Some like to do it after flowering, in the autumn, while others are happier doing it in the spring.

The scales should be dealt with as soon as possible after removal. Using a pot or tray of cutting mixture (half humus-rich soil, half sharp sand or grit), the scales should be planted so that their tops are just showing above the soil. The tray or pot should then be put into a warm glasshouse or propagator unit within the glasshouse until growth is seen.

Another method is to put the scales mixed with the soil into a polythene bag and place the bag in a warm position. Once the bulblets have been formed and roots start to appear the bag should be brought out into the light. Once the roots begin to grow and the first leaves begin to show, the scales should be potted up individually or lined out in rows in the garden, after a suitable hardening off period.

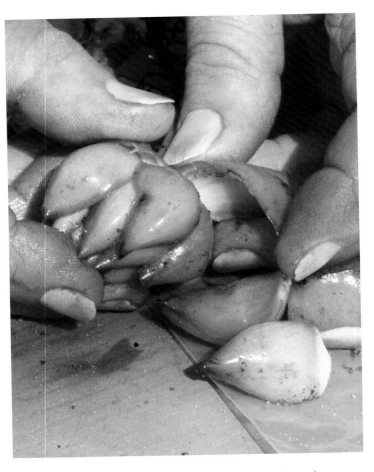

ABOVE *A* Lilium speciosum *bulb being scaled; the scales must be snapped off cleanly near the base.*
~

Keep the bulblets in growth for as long as possible before they die back for the winter by providing them with moisture and an occasional weak liquid feed. Bulbs of flowering size can be achieved in a couple of years but the majority are likely to take between three and five years before they flower.

DIVISION

This method of propagation is mainly used for the American stoloniferous or rhizomatous bulbs which can easily be split. Division is usually undertaken in the autumn while there is still some warmth to allow the plants to re-establish.

The detachable bulbs may be close to, or part of, the parent bulb or on a stoloniferous or rhizomatous stem that radiates from it. In either case the process is a very simple one in that the smaller bulbs are carefully split away from the parent and then replanted or, if required, potted up.

BULBLETS

Bulblets are formed on the underground part of the stem. They can be encouraged by deep planting of the stem-rooting lilies or by earthing them up with a good, leafmould-rich soil. In mid autumn the whole stem above the bulb can be removed and replanted with the bulblets still attached or the bulblets can be very carefully removed and planted out singly, either in the open garden or in pots.

BULBILS

Bulbils differ from bulblets in that they are produced on the stem *above* ground. They appear in the axils of the leaves of a few species and cultivars. Bulbils generally resemble small dark brown peas, perhaps a little elongated rather than completely round in shape. They can easily be removed from the plant and lined out in rows in a well-prepared seed bed, lightly covered with soil. Alternatively, they can be planted in pots or trays.

The bulbils will soon put out leaves and roots. Sometimes bulbils can be found still on the plants, with their roots developing; these can be removed with care and potted up or planted out as normal. While it is preferable to plant bulbils as soon as they are harvested, they will take a surprising amount of drying out before they lose their viability. They can therefore be sent through the post, suitably packed, to other growers.

Only a handful of lilies produce bulbils naturally, but others can be induced to do so by pinching out their flower buds before they become too well-formed. With so many other methods of reproduction available, the sacrifice of a year's flowers may not be considered worth the effort except for the gardener who likes to experiment. However, bulbils can provide a way of getting a large number of plants of a particular cultivar as, being a vegetative method of propagation, the resulting offspring are identical in flower to their parent, albeit after a wait of two to five years.

BELOW Bulbils are produced on the stem above the ground.

ABOVE Hybridizing by transferring pollen collected from the male parent onto the stigma of the female parent.

~

BELOW Pistil protectors are easily made by wrapping aluminium foil around the end of a pencil.

~

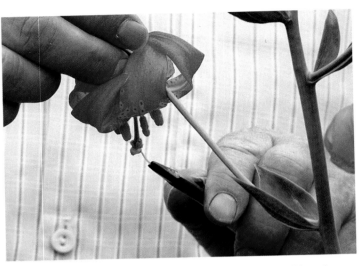

ABOVE Hybridizing – hand pollinating by rubbing the anther of the male parent onto the stigma of the female parent.

~

BELOW After pollinating the female parent, cover the stigma to protect it from contamination. Here pistil protectors are made from aliuminium foil.

~

HYBRIDIZATION

Much enjoyment can be obtained from deliberately crossing two different lilies in order to create a new one that has not existed before. The whole process can be undertaken in a light-hearted way, in a hit or miss manner, or it can be taken very seriously. The serious-minded hybridizer is more likely to meet with success, but the lighter-hearted could equally come up with a winner. Either way the grower must be prepared to be quite ruthless and only keep those plants that are worth keeping; the rest should be thrown away. There has been a tendency in amateur plant breeding to think that anything newly created is worth holding on to or,

worse still, giving away. This is not so, and because of this attitude many gardens contain inferior plants; only keep the best, throw the rest onto the compost heap.

The purpose of raising new forms can be to create new flower colours or to change some other characteristic. For example, a grower may wish to breed disease resistance into a particular form or to develop a form with shorter, more wind-resistant, stems. The parents must be selected carefully and the serious lily breeder should learn something about genetic inheritance. For the less serious breeder, different colour forms are the main attraction of hybridization and through experimentation he or she will begin to learn how to gain some control over the crosses.

Lilies are very easy plants to pollinate as all the sexual parts are large and easy to locate. The basic idea is to transfer pollen from a selected plant (the pollen or male parent) on to the plant that is to bear the seed (the seed or female parent).

A bud that is about to open on the plant chosen as the female parent should have its perianth segments (petals and sepals) eased open and all the male anthers should be removed with a pair of sharp, pointed scissors. Care should be taken not to cut off the female stigma. The purpose of removing the anthers is to ensure that the flower does not self-fertilize. The flower-head should then be covered with a cotton bag which will allow in air but not insects and stray pollen. Some growers now use polythene bags with holes pricked in them but others avoid them as they can produce a moist atmosphere conducive to introducing rot to the cut stamens. An alternative favoured by many growers is to encase just the stigma in a piece of silver foil, leaving the rest of the flower open to the air. After a couple of days the stigma will become shiny and sticky; this indicates that it is now receptive to pollen.

An anther should be removed from the male parent with a pair of tweezers and rubbed all over the stigma so that pollen sticks to the latter. The bag should then be replaced for a few days, in which time fertilization is carried out and the ovary begins to swell as the seeds develop. Once the petals have begun to wither the bag can be removed. The seed pod continues to develop until it is ripe and ready for harvesting. The techniques for harvesting seed are described below.

It is essential to tie a label to the flower-head that has been pollinated. This label should contain information about the two parents plus the date of pollination. All this information should also be recorded in a more permanent form in a notebook along with subsequent details of the results of the cross. This will teach the grower a great deal besides giving details of the parentage of the new offspring.

Both hands and tweezers should be sterilized with methylated spirits (wood alcohol) before moving on to the next plant.

Hybridization need not be confined to plants in your own garden. Anthers can be dried by packing them in a bottle or tube containing calcium chloride (a desiccator). The powder should be put in the bottom of the tube and kept in place with cotton wool. The anthers are placed on the cotton wool and then held in position with more cotton wool. The tube can then be sent to other growers. Another possibility is to put the tube in the warmest part of the refrigerator where it can be kept for up to two or even three months. It can then be used on plants that, under normal circumstances, could not possibly cross-pollinate with the male parent because they flower at different times.

COLLECTING SEED

Above SEED MUST BE DRIED BEFORE IT IS STORED FOR FUTURE PLANTING. THIS CAN BE DONE IN SIMPLE KITCHEN BOWLS AND CUPS.

Whether it is from a specially cross-pollinated plant or from other plants in the garden the grower should collect seed for own use and for giving to others.

When a lily seed pod is ripe it will begin to split from the top. Fortunately the shape of the pod means that the seed will not immediately fall to the ground which gives the grower a bit of grace, often several days. This means that he or she does not have to be as vigilant as growers of other, more difficult species, such as *Geranium*, which throw their seed in all directions the moment it ripens. The seed head can be cut off and placed or shaken into a paper bag. The bag can be left open in a cool airy place until the seed has dried. Once dried the seed should be cleaned (any remains of the seed pod or dust and dirt should be removed) and it can then be stored in a sealed envelope or other container until it is needed. Avoid leaving the seeds in the hot sun, on a glasshouse bench, for example.

Finally, do not forget to label the seed as soon as it is collected; unlabelled seed is worse than useless!

Below SEED CAN BE STORED IN AIRTIGHT JARS IN THE FREEZER FOR MANY YEARS.

PESTS AND DISEASES

L ilies seem to be more vulnerable to pests and diseases than many other garden plants. However, with attention and the very careful use of a few modern chemicals most should survive to put up a good show every year without too much bother.

It is unfortunate that chemical pesticides and fungicides are required as many gardeners are rightly beginning to be wary of them, for both safety and environmental reasons. In some cases they can be avoided, for example by killing aphids with fingers and thumbs rather than with a pesticide, but in other cases there really is no alternative if you want to save the plant. A wise gardener will only use chemicals when absolutely necessary and will *always* follow the instructions on the bottle or packet. Never exceed the given dosage as this will not increase the effectiveness of the chemical; it may well do the reverse and do more damage than the problem the chemical is supposed to control. It will also put more poisonous chemicals into the environment for no good reason.

A great deal can be achieved by examining all bulbs and lilies brought into the garden and rejecting any that show signs of pests or diseases. Good hygiene in clearing up any rotting material in the vicinity of the bulbs will also help to keep problems at bay.

PESTS

Aphids

Aphids (greenfly) always seem to be the number one trouble for garden plants, and they are for lilies too. They not only damage the green parts of the plant, but also cause indirect problems by acting as efficient carriers of viral diseases. This is because aphids feed by inserting their probosces into the nutrient-carrying vessels of the stem; the pressure in these vessels force-feeds the aphids. Any parts of the plant higher than the aphids receive less nourishment, and this can have serious consequences if many aphids attach themselves to one part of a plant. Aphids can be tackled by squashing them between finger and thumb, using tweezers on the more inaccessible parts of the plant. A more efficient way is to use one of the many proprietary brands of insecticide aimed at killing aphids. There are some, such as those based on pyrethrum or derris, which are made from naturally occurring chemical compounds.

LEFT Fasciation looks like multiple stems, flattened together. Note the increased number of flower buds in this fasciated Lilium davidii.

ABOVE *Insect damage to a lily bud.*

~

Lily beetles

Lily beetles are a scourge that affects mainland Europe and certain areas of southern England (especially around Surrey) but which have not yet, and hopefully never will, reach America. They are a nuisance both in the larval and adult stage, eating leaves and flowers with great gusto. The larvae are revolting to look at, being a grimy yellow and covered with a slimy secretion. The adult fares a bit better being bright red with black legs and antennae. As a precaution all lilies brought into the garden should be checked to make sure that there are no beetles, larvae or eggs, which can be found attached to the underside of the lower leaves. When seen, all three can be picked off the plant by hand, and this is one of the most effective countermeasures. Alternatively, the beetles can be sprayed or dusted with an insecticide based on malathion or gamma-HCH.

Lily thrips

Lily thrips attack the bulbs both as larvae and as adults. The larvae and adults are pink and black respectively and can be found mainly around the bases of the scales. If they are discovered or suspected of being on bulbs, the bulbs should be immersed in water at 44°C (111°F) for one hour or dusted or sprayed with an insecticide based on malathion or gamma-HCH.

Bulb mites

Bulb mites damage the bulb and its roots. They are very small and yellowish or pink in colour. The treatment is the same as that for lily thrips.

Leatherjackets, wireworms, swift moth larvae

Leatherjackets, wireworms, swift moth larvae and several other soil-borne larvae can be a nuisance as they eat into bulbs and chew through roots. Gamma-HCH can be incorporated into the soil around the bulbs as a preventative measure if there are numbers of the pest present. In light soils the larvae can be riddled out by hand when preparing the ground for planting.

Slugs and snails

Slugs and snails are other universal pests that do damage, not only to the bulbs but to all other parts of the plant as well, by chewing them. Slug bait (an organic one being preferable) can be used following the maker's directions. Alternatively, the slugs and snails can be picked off by hand; this is best done at night by torchlight. After collecting for a number of nights in a row the predators can be reduced to acceptable numbers without the need for bait.

FUNGAL DISEASES

Botrytis

Botrytis, once known as lily disease, is a rot or blight that first shows up as dark spots on the leaves, particularly in damp seasons. The spots turn white and spread up the stems to other leaves and the flower. The top growth usually dies off but the disease rarely affects the bulb below ground. As soon as botrytis is noticed the affected leaves should be removed (and burnt) and the rest of the plant sprayed with a fungicide; with luck the year's flowering

ABOVE *Botrytis begins as circular brown spots on leaves; eventually the entire leaf turns brown.*

~

capacity of the plant should not be impaired. In wet seasons evasive action can be taken by spraying the plant with Bordeaux mixture or a colloidal copper fungicide. Also spray the surrounding soil to kill off any spores.

Basal rot

Basal rot is a fusarium disease that attacks the scales where they are attached to the basal plate, killing the whole bulb. Once in the soil basal rot is likely to persist for some years and it is not advisable to plant any more lilies in the same ground unless the soil has been cleared of the disease by treating it with two per cent formalin solution. It is likely that any disease will originally be brought into the garden on infected bulbs, so inspect them for the rot. Any badly affected bulbs or the remains of bulbs should be burnt. Those that are in the first stages can often be restored by dipping them in 0.5 per cent benomyl solution.

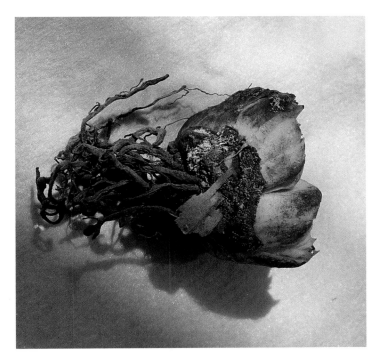

ABOVE Blue mould on a bulb.

~

Blue mould

Blue mould is caused by a penicilin fungus. It is first noticed as brown spots eating into the scales. As these enlarge they turn white, eventually turning a bluish colour as the spores develop. Badly affected bulbs should be burnt, while those in the first stages can have the affected scales removed and burnt.

Rhizoctonia

Rhizoctonia attacks damaged or dying parts of the bulb below ground. Badly affected bulbs should be burnt, while milder cases can be treated with a fungicide.

VIRUS DISEASES

Unfortunately, lilies suffer from more than their fair share of virus diseases. Aphids are one of the commonest carriers and they should be strictly controlled. Planting lilies in mixed or shrub borders often helps to contain any disease as the other plants form natural barriers to the aphids. There is little one can do about infected plants except burn them; therefore the differences between the various viruses are a little academic. However, the commonest are described so that the gardener will at least recognize them.

ABOVE Cucumber mosaic virus evidenced by streaking on the leaves.

~

Cucumber mosaic

Cucumber mosaic first shows itself by streaked or mottled leaves followed by distortion. Flowers and stems also become distorted.

ABOVE Lily mottle virus has caused the colour variations in this lily flower.

~

RIGHT Lily mottle virus is seen as mottling on the leaves and buds.

~

Lily mottle

Lily mottle is similar in appearance and effect to cucumber mosaic. The same virus produces the colour breaks that are considered attractive in tulips, so these two types of plant should be kept as far apart as possible.

Lily symptomless virus

Lily symptomless virus tends to make plants languish and eventually die out without showing any real symptoms of a disease.

Lily rosette or yellowflat

Lily rosette or yellowflat causes the lilies to become stunted with the leaves being produced too close together. The leaves also curve downwards and turn yellow. The flowers either do not develop beyond the bud stage or they are distorted.

OTHER DISORDERS

As if the above were not enough, there are a few other disorders from which lilies can suffer.

Chlorosis

Chlorosis occurs when acid-loving lilies are grown on alkaline soils and manifests itself in yellow leaves. The problem can be overcome by watering the soil with chelated iron, although a better solution would be either not to grow this type of lily on alkaline soil, or to create raised beds (or use pots) in which the pH of the soil can be controlled.

Drought

Drought is signalled by flagging, limp leaves. Immediate watering will remedy the situation, but consider incorporating more moisture-retentive humus into the soil and/or mulching.

BELOW *Fasciation looks like multiple stems, flattened together. Note the increased number of flower buds in this fasciated* Lilium davidii.
~

Bad drainage

Bad drainage should never be allowed to happen, but when it does brown streaks appear on the leaves which eventually shrivel. Install proper drainage over the whole area if necessary or incorporate more grit into the soil if it is just a local problem. Avoid creating sumps under the plant.

Frost

Frost can cause damage similar to virus diseases, but is not usually fatal. There is not much that can be done about it, except to avoid planting in frost pockets.

Fasciation

Fasciation creates interesting but ugly plants that usually intrigue people. It is caused by damage to the young growth and, as the stem grows, it looks as though two or more stems have been joined together forming a grotesque flattened stem. The number of flowers that each stem bears is increased, but they are smaller than in normal plants. The plant will return to its normal appearance the following season.

This is not a complete list, but it covers all species that are readily available. Other species are only likely to be grown by more advanced growers.

In this list the perianth segments, ie the similar-looking petals and sepals, are all referred to as petals.

LEFT A richly coloured Bellingham Hybrid, which can also appear in shades of yellow and red. This lily is an old hybrid, and is particularly virus-resistant.
~

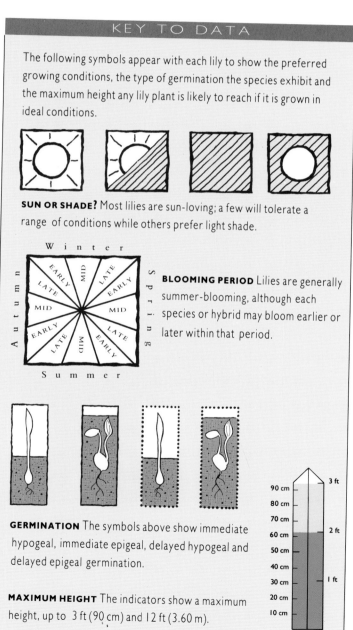

KEY TO DATA

The following symbols appear with each lily to show the preferred growing conditions, the type of germination the species exhibit and the maximum height any lily plant is likely to reach if it is grown in ideal conditions.

SUN OR SHADE? Most lilies are sun-loving; a few will tolerate a range of conditions while others prefer light shade.

BLOOMING PERIOD Lilies are generally summer-blooming, although each species or hybrid may bloom earlier or later within that period.

GERMINATION The symbols above show immediate hypogeal, immediate epigeal, delayed hypogeal and delayed epigeal germination.

MAXIMUM HEIGHT The indicators show a maximum height, up to 3 ft (90 cm) and 12 ft (3.60 m).

Lilium amabile
~

A free-flowering, Turk's-cap lily with pendant red flowers, spotted with black. It comes from Korea and will grow in a wide range of soils, being happy in either sun or partial shade. The

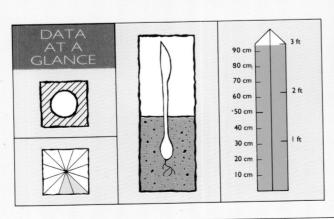

flowers are produced from early to mid summer on stems up to 3 ft (90 cm) tall. It is a stem-rooting species and the seed has immediate epigeal germination. There is a yellow variety *L. a. luteum*.

DATA
AT A
GLANCE

90 cm — 3 ft
80 cm
70 cm
60 cm — 2 ft
·50 cm
40 cm
30 cm — 1 ft
20 cm
10 cm

Lilium auratum

L. auratum
~

Known as the Japanese gold-ray lily, this species is one of the glories of the genus. It has large, sometimes huge (up to 12 in/ 30 cm across), bowl-shaped flowers which are not only wonderfully fragrant, but also very numerous, with up to 30 blooms per stem. The true plant has white flowers with a gold stripe (the 'auratum' of the name) on each petal and is spotted with red. There are also a number of cultivars of various colours. The flowers appear from late summer into autumn on stems that grow up to 6 ft (1.80 m) tall. It is a stem-rooting species and has delayed epigeal germination. Unfortunately, it is not tolerant of alkaline conditions, but it makes a splendid pot specimen, which is the best way to grow it in limy areas. It is rather prone to virus diseases so bulbs should only come from accredited sources.

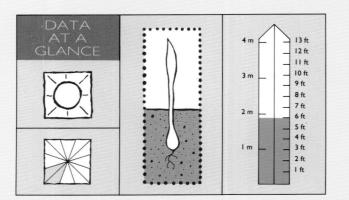

L. bolanderi
~

A species from the western United States with funnel-shaped flowers of a deep red merging into a yellow throat. The inner part of the petals are also spotted with purple. These flowers appear in mid summer on stems that reach up to 3 ft (90 cm). It is not a stem-rooting lily and has delayed hypogeal germination. Unfortunately it is not long-lived and needs to be regularly resown to keep it going. Plant in a sunny position, preferably in a humus-rich soil; however, this lily can be grown on alkaline conditions.

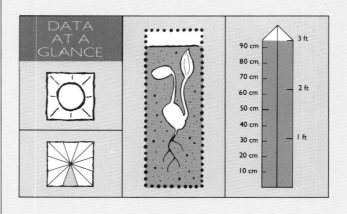

L. bulbiferum
~

From Europe, this species, the orange lily, has upward-facing, cup-shaped flowers, and orange-red petals with dark spots. The flowers are produced from early to mid summer and the stems rise up to 5ft (1.50 m). It is a stem-rooting species and also has bulbils in its axils. Germination is delayed hypogeal. The species is tolerant of a wide range of soils. Better known than its species is the variety *L. bulbiferum croceum*, which has paler, orange flowers. Even better known, perhaps, are the Mid-Century Hybrids (see A–Z of hybrids), of which several have become named forms.

This lily species hybridizes easily and it is a good plant with which to start for anyone wishing to try this technique.

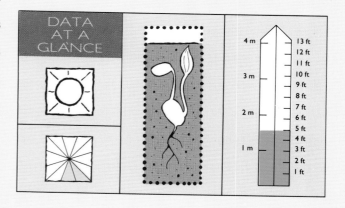

DATA AT A GLANCE

L. canadense

~

This was one of the earliest of the American lilies to be introduced into Europe. It is a tall species, up to 6ft (1.80 m) high, that carries a mass of downward-facing, trumpet-shaped flowers. The recurved yellow petals are speckled with dark spots at their base. Flowering takes place in mid summer. This is not an easy species in that it dislikes both limy soils and winter wet. At the same time it will not tolerate too dry a position, needing plenty of moisture when it is in flower. This lily is a stoloniferous one and has a few stem roots. Its germination is delayed hypogeal. There are several varieties with darker coloured flowers.

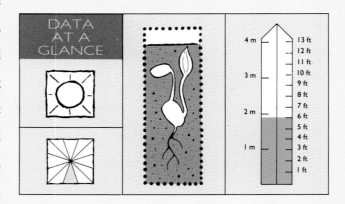

Lilium candidum

L. candidum
~

This species, the Madonna lily, is one of the oldest in cultivation as shown by paintings of it which appear in remains from Minoan Crete dating from the 15th century BC. The species originates in southeastern Europe and the adjacent areas of Asia. Its 5ft (1.50 m) stems carry up to 20 pure-white flowers, set off by anthers covered in golden pollen and emitting the most wonderful fragrance. The flowers are funnel-shaped, their flared mouths pointing straight out. This is a lily that likes limy soils, although care should be taken by adding humus to make certain that the soil does not dry out too much. The Madonna lily differs from most others in that it must be planted shallowly, with its growing tip either at or just below soil level. It should be planted in full sun where air can circulate freely around it. Several hybrids have been produced from Madonna lilies, the best, and earliest, being *L.* × *testaceum*, the Nankeen lily.

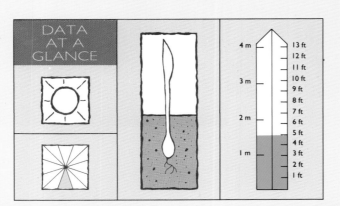

L. cernuum
~

This is a delicate, little, Turk's-cap lily from northeastern Asia that only grows to 2 ft (60 cm) or so. The scented flowers are a deep rich pink, marked with purple spots. They appear from early to mid summer. The species produces stem roots and seed which has immediate epigeal germination. The bulb is not very long-lived, and so the plant needs propagating regularly to ensure its survival. It grows well in rock gardens and is tolerant of lime.

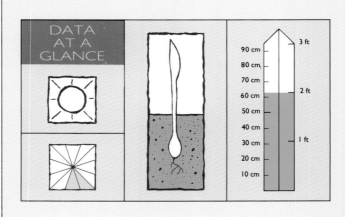

L. chalcedonicum
~

A lovely Turk's-cap lily from Greece with a rather curious smell.
The flowers are a bright red and appear from mid to late summer.
It is quite a tall species, reaching up to 5 ft (1.50 m). It is stem-
rooting with seed that is immediate epigeal germinating if sown
fresh, otherwise delays can be expected. It is a short-lived species,
so should be propagated regularly. *L. chalcedonicum* will grow
under limy conditions and tolerate quite a bit of shade. It is the
other parent, with *L. candidum*, of *L.* × *testaceum*.

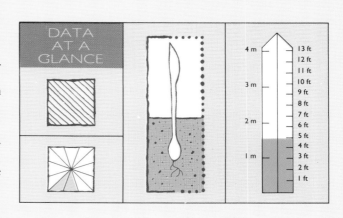

L. columbianum
~

This is one of the most widespread of the American species, found right along the western coast. It can be a floriferous plant with many nodding Turk's-cap flowers in a range of oranges, with purple spots, especially strong towards the throat. The plant will grow up to 5 ft (1.50 m) tall and is quite adaptable as it likes either sun or shade and will be happy in a wide range of soils. It flowers in mid summer. Germination is delayed hypogeal.

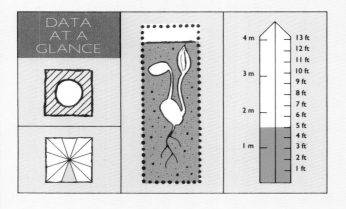

L. concolor
~

A delightful lily from the Far East which grows up to 3 ft (90 cm) high. It has fragrant, star-shaped flowers that open their orange-red petals towards the sky. The flowers appear from early to mid summer and can comprise up to ten per stem. *L. concolor* will enjoy full sun or light shade and can be grown in lime-rich soils. Being short, it can be grown in a rock garden or as a pot specimen. Seed germination is immediate epigeal. There is a variety, *L. concolor* var. *pulchellum*, that has spotted flowers.

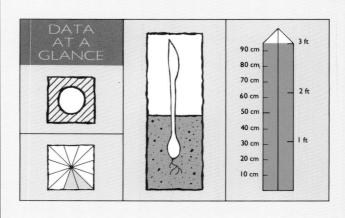

L. dauricum
~

An upward-facing lily, which has played an important role in the history of hybridization. This species comes from Russia and northeastern Asia. The cup-shaped flowers, which are produced from early to mid summer, are orangey red, shading to a deep yellow towards the centre, and are spotted with deep red. This is a stoloniform species which produces stem roots. The stems themselves only reach 2–3 ft (60–90 cm) high. Germination is immediate epigeal. The species will take either full sun or light shade and does best in lime-free conditions. There is a shorter form *L. dauricum* var. *alpinum*.

L. davidii
~

This Chinese lily comes from the west of the country. It produces up to 20 Turk's-cap flowers, each orange-red in colour with deep purple spots. It is easily grown from seed (immediate epigeal germination) and hybridizes readily, giving many hybrids and strains in cultivation; indeed, the true wild plant is rarely seen. It flowers from mid to late summer. *L. davidii* is a stem-rooting plant that will grow up to 5 ft (1.50 m) or more in some of its varieties such as *macranthum*. It will just about tolerate limy soils as long as humus has been added.

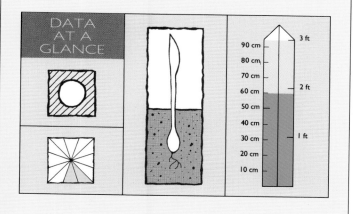

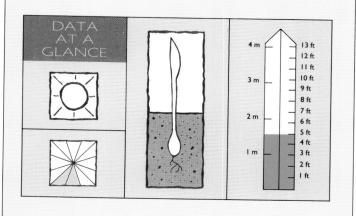

L. formosanum
~

As its name suggests, this lily comes from Taiwan (formerly Formosa). It has beautiful outward-facing, trumpet-shaped flowers that appear in the late summer and early autumn. It is not a very long-lived lily, but to offset this it comes very readily from seed, with immediate epigeal germination. Indeed, it can even flower within a year of sowing. The flowers are white on the inside and flushed with a dark reddish pink on the outside. The plant will grow up to 6 ft (1.80 m) tall, but on the other hand it may remain as short as 6 in (15 cm), particularly in the variety *pricei*. The latter flowers slightly earlier than the true species and its diminutive size makes it an excellent rock garden plant. The true species and *L. formosarum* var. *pricei* are both stem rooters and will tolerate lime.

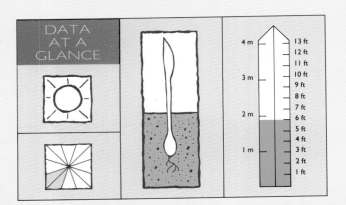

L. hansonii
~

This species is rare in the wild, coming from only one island in the Sea of Japan, but is common in cultivation. It has up to 12 Turk's-cap flowers, each coloured orange with brown-purple spots towards the centre. Each petal is thick, almost like orange peel. *L. hansonii* has a wonderful scent and makes a good cut flower. It flowers around mid summer and grows up to 5 ft (1.50 m) tall. It is stem-rooting and is a robust plant that is reasonably resistant to virus infections. The species will grow in either sun or light shade and will grow on limy soils. Germination is delayed hypogeal and can be erratic.

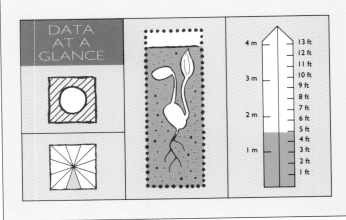

L. henryi
~

Not to be confused with the totally different *L. henrici*, this lily is another Turk's-cap species with up to 20 flowers per stem. It is a vigorous, hardy, long-lived plant with orange flowers that have dark spots and a green stripe down the nectary furrows. The flowers appear in late summer on stems that can reach, in favourable circumstances, up to 10 ft (3 m). This lily grows on limestone in the wild and does well on it in cultivation. Lime may be added to acid or neutral soils. *L. henryi* will grow in light shade and germination is immediate epigeal.

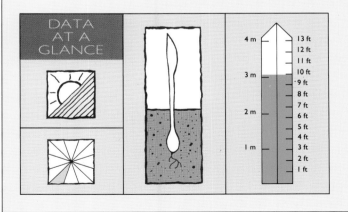

L. humboldtii
~

This is a Californian lily which carries sometimes quite large numbers of Turk's-cap flowers in mid summer. A bright orange, speckled with maroon spots, they have the added advantage of being fragrant. These are carried on stems that can reach up to 8 ft (2.5 m) high. The bulbs are sub-rhizomatous and lack stem roots. It has a variety, *L. h.* var. *occelatum* (illustrated), which does have these stem roots, as well as having spots that are ringed in crimson, reaching right to the tips of the petals. Both produce seed that has delayed hypogeal germination. Plant out in a very well-drained soil in either sun or light shade.

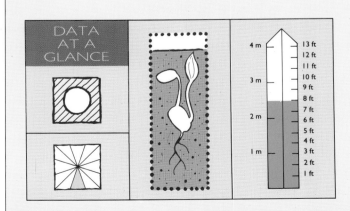

L. iridollae

~

A Turk's-cap species from the south-east United States. The flowers are yellow with brown spots and appear from mid to late summer on stems that can reach up to 6½ ft (2 m) in height. The bulbs are stoloniferous and there are stem roots present. Germination is immediate hypogeal. It grows in a moist soil in full sun or light shade.

L. kelloggii

~

A western American Turk's-cap species, which has up to 20 blooms per stem, although some vigorous plants will well exceed this number. The colour varies from white to mauve-pink with a yellow band towards the throat. There are purple spots at the base of the petals. The flowering time is from mid to late summer. The bulb is rhizomatous and the plant's stem reaches up to 4 ft (1.20 m) high. Germination is delayed hypogeal. *L. kelloggii* does best in a shady position in a gritty soil that does not dry out.

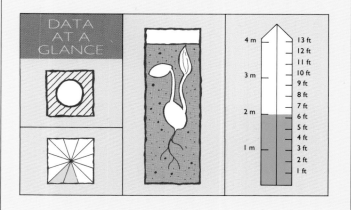

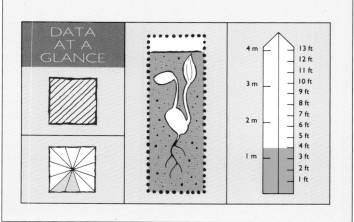

L. lancifolium
~

This is the famous tiger lily from the Far East. Debate still rages over the name as it has long been known as *L. tigrinum* and many people wish it so to remain, but it is now generally accepted that it should be called *L. lancifolium*. It is a floriferous plant with up to 20 or more (even up to 40 on some specimens) Turk's-cap flowers. These are orange-red in colour with dark purple spotting. There are a whole range of varieties which have flowers of varying colours from yellow (var. *flaviflorum*) to bright orange-red (var. *splendens*). There is also a double form and one with variegated leaves. The plants flower from late summer to early autumn, and reach up to 7 ft (2 m) tall. The species has stem roots and the germination is of the immediate epigeal type. It can also be propagated from bulbils. *L. lancifolium* prefers an acid or neutral soil, but will grow on those with an alkaline tendency.

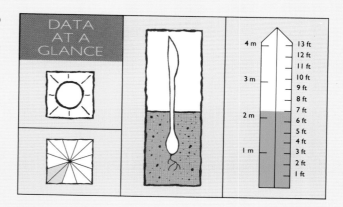

L. lankongense

~

This lily comes from China and Tibet and is important because of the number of hybrids it has spawned in recent years. The species itself is a difficult plant to grow and is prone to virus disease. It is a Turk's-cap variety in varying shades of pink with red-purple spotting. The fragrant flowers appear during mid summer. It grows up to 4 ft (1.20 m) tall and is stem-rooting. The bulb is stoloniform, and seed germination is immediate epigeal. *L. lankongense* grows best on a neutral or acid soil but it will tolerate alkaline conditions. It will grow in full sun or, if conditions are hot, light shade.

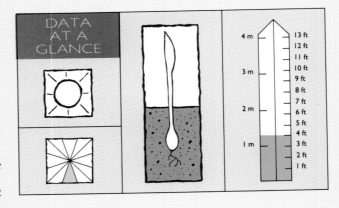

DATA AT A GLANCE

L. longiflorum
~

Known as either the Easter lily or the Bermuda lily, this is one of the most popular of lilies with the cut-flower trade. The vernacular name Bermuda is misleading as it in fact comes from Japan, although for many years Bermuda was one of the main exporters of this lily as a cut flower. The reason for this species's popularity lies with its pure white, fragrant trumpets which it produces during mid summer or throughout the year under glass if it is forced. Another reason for its popularity with gardeners is that it can be induced to flower from seed in as little as six months, very rapid indeed for lilies. The germination, as one would gather from this, is immediate epigeal. *L. longiflorum* is considered tender in many areas and is often grown in pots or under glass. It can,

however, be grown outside if given free drainage and protection from frosts. It is stem-rooting, the portion above ground reaching up to 3 ft (90 cm) tall, and is lime tolerant. There are quite a number of named cultivars for the keen gardener to explore.

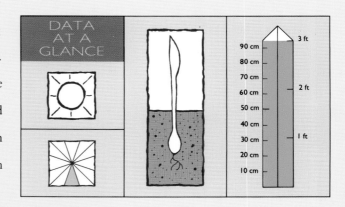

L. mackliniae
~

This species was not introduced into cultivation until just after the Second World War when Frank Kingdon-Ward sent home seed from Manipur, now in Bangladesh. It is a beautiful species with nodding bell-shaped flowers that are a pinkish purple on the inside and darker on the outer surfaces of the petals. Flowering takes place during early to mid summer. It is a stem-rooting species that grows up to 3 ft (90 cm) tall. Germination is immediate epigeal. It is a bit tender and might need protection, but otherwise it is easy to grow as long as it has a neutral or acid soil and light shade.

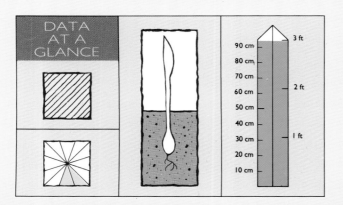

L. maritimum
~

As its name implies, this species, the coast lily, is found in regions that border the sea, along the coast of California, for example. The pendant flowers are funnel-shaped, varying in colour from orange-red to deep red, speckled with deep maroon spots. It is a short species varying in height from a few inches occasionally to 3 ft (90 cm) and has flowers which appear from early to late summer. The more vigorous plants may carry up to 20 flowers per stem. It has a rhizomatous bulb and is not stem-rooting. Germination is delayed hypogeal. This species prefers a light soil enriched with humus and a lightly shaded position.

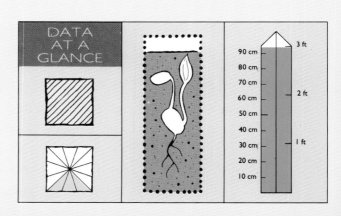

L. martagon

~

This is one of the oldest lilies in cultivation and has remained popular ever since its first introduction sometime way back in history. It has the greatest range of all lilies, being found in most countries of both Europe and Asia. While not native to Britain, it can be seen growing wild as a garden escapee in quite a number of places. It is the most classic of the Turk's-cap-shaped lilies. Its colour varies from pink to dark purple, often with dark spotting. There are a number of named colour forms of which the most pleasing to many people is the white *L. martagon* var. *album*. The flower's one drawback is its smell, which can be considered unpleasant. The plant flowers from early to mid summer. The martagon lily can grow quite tall, up to 6 ft (1.80 m), and can have as many as 40 flowers or more per stem on an established plant under the right conditions. There are stem roots and the seed has delayed hypogeal germination. *L. martagon* will grow in a variety of positions including quite dense shade and on a variety of soils including alkaline ones. When satisfied it will self-sow (albeit taking several years to reach flowering size), making it a good plant for naturalizing in the wilder parts of the garden.

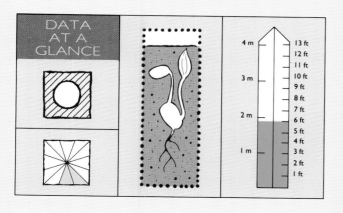

DATA AT A GLANCE

L. michiganense
~

This is a species from the eastern United States. The flowers are Turk's-cap in shape and vary in colour from orange to red, spotted in a deeper red or purple. These are borne from early to mid summer on stems that reach up to 5 ft (1.50 m) high. The bulb is stoloniferous and there are no stem roots present. The seed has delayed hypogeal germination. Plant out in a moisture-retentive soil in full sun.

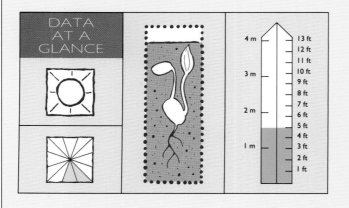

L. monadelphum
~

Confusion reigns between this and *L. szovitsianum* in that some authorities consider the two plants as just geographic variants of the same species while others consider them botanically distinct. From our point of view it does not matter whether they are separate or all lumped under *L. monadelphum* as to the majority of gardeners they are the same plant. The species hails from the Caucasus and Turkey and has pendulous yellow flowers with purple spotting. The flowers have a strong fragrance and appear in early summer. The stems can reach up to 6 ft (1.80 m) and carry up to 30 blooms each on well-established plants, although five to six is the norm. There are a few stem roots and the seed germination is delayed hypogeal. *L. monadelphum* will grow on a wide range of soils and prefers a partially shaded position. The bright yellow flowers make this species a good lily to grow amongst shrubs as the yellow stands out well against green foliage.

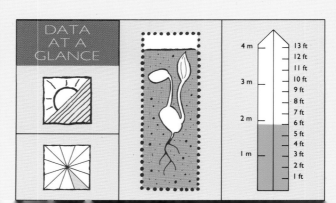

L. nepalense

~

As its name suggests, this beautiful species comes from Nepal, but it is also found elsewhere along the Himalayas. It has pendant greenish-yellow flowers that are purple in the throat. They are funnel-shaped with reflexed petals. Unfortunately, this species' beauty is a little marred by its smell which some people find unpleasant. It is an early flowering species, from late spring into early summer. The stems can reach up to 3 ft (90 cm) high. The bulb is stoloniferous and it is stem-rooting. Seed has immediate epigeal germination. *L. nepalense* is slightly tender and may need winter protection if grown in the open. If grown in a glasshouse it is best to plant it in a bed rather than a pot, so that its stoloniferous roots can wander. It prefers a neutral to acid soil.

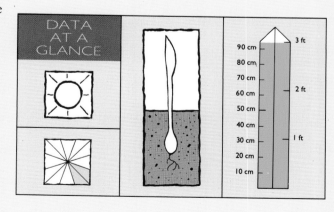

DATA AT A GLANCE

90 cm — 3 ft
80 cm
70 cm
60 cm — 2 ft
50 cm
40 cm
30 cm — 1 ft
20 cm
10 cm

L. pardalinum

~

This species from the western side of the United States is known as the leopard lily or panther lily. It is robust, hardy, and of great stature, rising up to 8 ft (2.40 m) tall. The flowers are of the Turk's-cap variety, their colour varying from crimson at the recurved petal tips to orange at the centre. They also have reddish-brown spots. Flowering time is around mid summer. This species does not have roots on the stems. Germination is delayed hypogeal. Although it will tolerate lime, *L. pardalinum* grows best on a soil that is moisture-retentive. It makes a wonderful cut flower. There is a natural variant, *L. pardalinum* var. *giganteum*, which is a very vigorous plant with up to 50 blooms on stems that can reach 10 ft (3 m) high. There are several other forms available.

L. occidentale

~

This is a rare lily from the western United States that bears nodding Turk's-cap flowers coloured crimson shading to orange in the throat, with purple spots. They are carried on stems that grow up to 6 ft (1.80 m) in height and appear around mid summer. Germination is delayed hypogeal. Plant out in a moisture-retentive soil in sun or part shade.

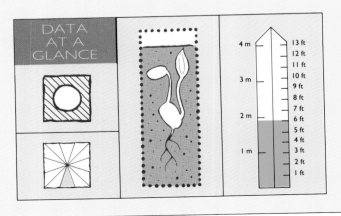

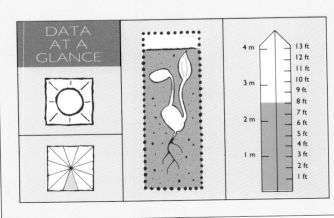

Lilium pardalinum

L. parryi
~

Another lily from western America, this time with trumpet-shaped flowers. The blossoms are a citrous yellow with a touch of dark spotting in the throat, and delicately scented. They appear during mid summer. *L. parryi* is quite a tall species, growing up to 6 ft (1.80 m) high. The bulb is rhizomatous. The seed has immediate hypogeal germination. This lily does not like stagnant air as it is prone to fungal attack, and, therefore, should be planted where air can circulate freely. Although it does not like moist air, it does like moist soil and should be planted in such conditions, although, of course, the soil must not become waterlogged.

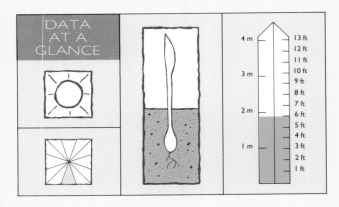

DATA AT A GLANCE

L. parvum
~

This lily comes from the western United States. Its name (*parvum* means small) derives not from its stature, which reaches up to 6 ft (1.80 m) in suitable conditions, but from the size of the flowers, which must be one of the smallest of all the lily species. They are bell-shaped and face outwards. The colour varies from orange to red, with purplish spots, and the plants come into flower around mid summer. The bulb is rhizomatous. There is a lack of stem roots. Germination is delayed hypogeal. *L. parvum* will grow on a range of soils but prefers a free-draining one with extra humus added, preferably in a lightly shaded position.

L. philadelphicum
~

This species comes from eastern North America where it has a variety of vernacular names including flame lily, glade lily, orange cup lily, red lily and wood lily. These give an indication of its shape, colour and habitat. It has upward-facing, cup-shaped flowers with a colour that varies from orange to flame red-orange. The stems grow up to 3 ft (90 cm) high and root below ground level. Germination can be either immediate or delayed epigeal. In the wild *L. philadephicum* grows in woodland areas and therefore appreciates a lightly shaded position although it will grow in full sun. It also prefers a neutral or acid soil with plenty of humus, as, again, befits its woodland home. It is parent to quite a number of cultivated forms.

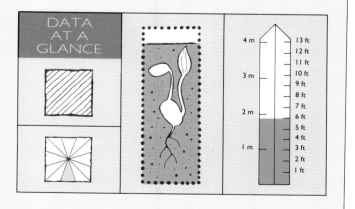

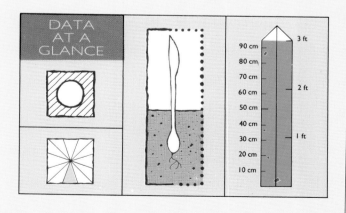

L. pumilum
~

Sometimes known as *L. tenuifolium*, this lily is one of the smaller forms, normally growing to only 18 in (45 cm) high. Eastern Asia is its natural home. It has dainty, scented flowers of a Turk's-cap shape. The petals are scarlet and slightly perfumed. In spite of its diminutive height, it is a vigorous species, sometimes producing up to 20 flowers per stem or even more on odd occasions. The flowers appear from early to mid summer. *L. pumilum* is stem-rooting and has immediate epigeal germination. It is not a long-lived lily, but as it produces copious amounts of seed there is little problem with keeping it going. It prefers a sunny position (perhaps on a rock garden) and lime-free soil, although it will grow in limy soil which has been well treated with humus.

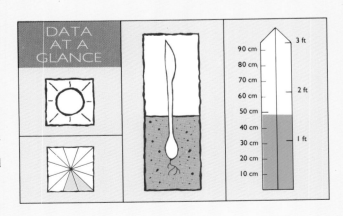

DATA AT A GLANCE

90 cm — 3 ft
80 cm
70 cm
60 cm — 2 ft
50 cm
40 cm
30 cm — 1 ft
20 cm
10 cm

L. pyrenaicum
~

As its name suggests this lily comes from the Pyrenees. It is a popular lily, partly because of its bright colour and partly because it is an easy, hardy plant to grow. The flower's shape is that of a Turk's-cap and its colour is a bright greenish yellow set off against the narrow green leaves. The petals are marked with deep red spots and streaks. The orange pollen on the anthers also makes a strong contrasting feature. Flowering time is from late spring to early summer. It is not a stem-rooting species. The stem itself will grow up to 4 ft (1.20 m) tall in favourable conditions. Seed germination is delayed epigeal. L. pyrenaicum is easy to grow from seed and tolerates a wide range of soils. There are quite a number of different named forms that are worth exploring.

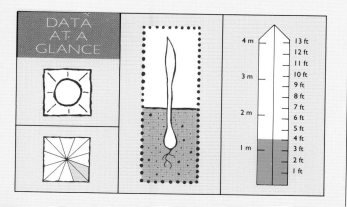

L. regale
~

A very beautiful and justifiably popular lily, very easy to grow as it has a robust constitution. Surprisingly it was not introduced into cultivation until 1903 when it was discovered by the plant hunter EH Wilson in southwest China. Its wonderful trumpet-shaped flowers (up to 20 or 30 per stem) are pure white in colour with a rose pink tinge to the buds and outside of the petals. The species flowers from early to mid summer. As well as its beautiful appearance L. regale has a marvellous fragrance. It grows up to 6 ft (1.80 m) tall on stems that root below soil level. Germination is of the immediate epigeal type. The species is easy to grow in any soil, although it will not do quite so well on lime. As to position, it is again versatile, prefering a sunny spot but tolerating light shade. Needless to say, such a good lily has produced a number of cultivars and hybrids. One of the best is the pure white (with no pink on the reverse of the petals) cultivar, 'Album'.

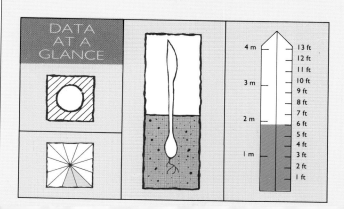

L. rubellum
~

This is a lily of great charm from Japan. The flowers are funnel-shaped and of a delicate shell pink, which is set off well by the shiny green leaves. The flowers appear in early summer and are sweetly scented. *L. rubellum* is not a very tall plant reaching up to only 2 ft (60 cm) or a little more. It is stem-rooting and germination is delayed hypogeal. It prefers a moist, lime-free soil in a partially shaded position.

L. rubescens
~

A beautiful lily from the western United States, it is also known as the chapparal lily or redwood lily. Although it has been in cultivation for well over a century, *L. rubescens* is still not frequently seen in gardens. The very fragrant flowers are trumpet-shaped and of pale lilac colour darkening to a purplish pink, finely spotted with purple. It is a vigorous lily with up to 30 blooms per stem, the latter growing up to 6 ft (1.80 m). The flowering season is around mid summer. It is a rhizomatous species and the stem is non-rooting. The seed has delayed hypogeal germination. *L. rubescens* grows on a range of soils and prefers a sunny position with shaded roots.

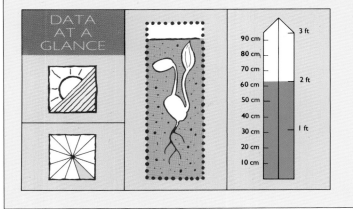

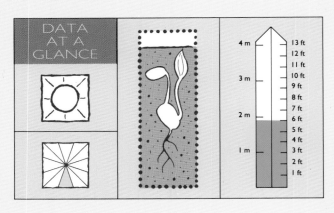

L. speciosum
~

A very fragrant species that comes mainly from Japan. It has a pendant flower with strongly recurved petals. They are white suffused with pink darkening towards the base and speckled with darker spots. There are many varieties and cultivars which ring the changes on these colours, but the true species takes quite a lot of beating. The exposed style and stamens with their anthers covered in brown pollen add to the quality of this lily. It flowers in early autumn and in cooler areas it might be best to grow it in pots to allow it to flower to its full potential. Stems reach up to 5–6 ft (1.50–1.80 m). *L. speciosum* is stem-rooting and has delayed hypogeal germination. This species is a confirmed lime-hater that will grow in either a sunny or light shady position.

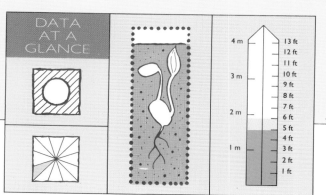

DATA AT A GLANCE

4 m — 13 ft
12 ft
11 ft
3 m — 10 ft
9 ft
8 ft
7 ft
2 m — 6 ft
5 ft
4 ft
1 m — 3 ft
2 ft
1 ft

L. superbum

~

This species comes from the eastern side of the United States. It is a vigorous lily with up to 40 flowers per stem. These flowers are nodding Turk's-caps, coloured orange merging with crimson towards the tips of the petals, and to green towards the base. There are also a few maroon spots. The flowers are scented and occur from late summer into autumn on stems that reach up to 8 ft (2.40 m) or more. The bulbs are stoloniferous and are stem-rooting. The germination is delayed hypogeal. This lily requires a lime-free soil that is free-draining but never dries out, and a light shady position.

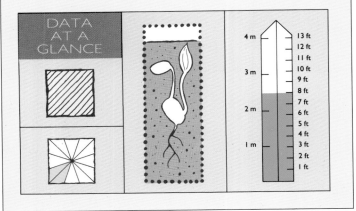

L. taliense

~

This delightful Chinese lily has fragrant Turk's-cap flowers, each white, spattered with purple spots. The flowers appear in mid summer on stems that rise up to 4 ft (1.20 m) high. It is a stoloniferous lily with rooting stems. Germination is immediate epigeal. This is a short-lived species and should be resown regularly to ensure continuance. Plant out in a part-shady position, preferably in acid soil.

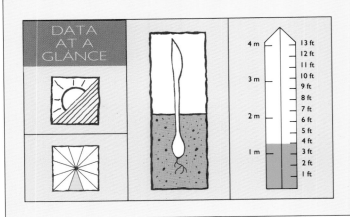

L. tsingtauense

~

Although part of the martagon group of lilies, this Chinese species has flared, cup-shaped flowers that are upward facing. The thick petals are an orange-red and spotted with maroon. The flowers appear in mid summer on stems that reach up to 3 ft (90 cm) in height. This is a non stem-rooting lily which has delayed hypogeal germination. It prefers an acid soil enriched with humus and either a part-shaded or a sunny position.

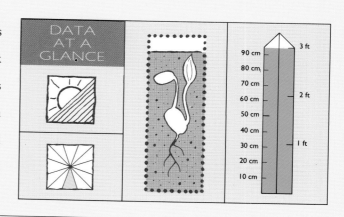

DATA AT A GLANCE

90 cm — 3 ft
80 cm
70 cm — 2 ft
60 cm
50 cm
40 cm
30 cm — 1 ft
20 cm
10 cm

L. wallichianum

~

This funnel-shaped lily comes from the Himalayas. The flowers are creamy-white, suffused with green on the outside of the petals. They are fragrant and appear during the early autumn on stems that grow up to 6 ft (1.80 m) tall. The bulb is stoloniferous with a rooting stem. Seed germination is immediate epigeal. This lily tends to be a bit tender and is best grown under glass, at least in colder areas, but it will need plenty of room for its stoloniferous stems to run. If planted outside it likes a well-drained soil with plenty of grit and humus. This lily is quite rare in cultivation although it is now becoming commercially available.

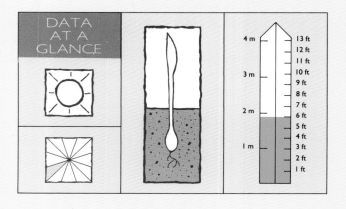

L. washingtonianum

~

This species of lily from the western United States has fragrant flowers which are funnel-shaped and outward-facing. The flowers are pure white, adding a touch of lilac as they fade, with purple spots towards the throat. On vigorous plants there can be up to 18 or 20 blooms per stem, which reaches up to 8 ft (2.40 m) high in some cases. Flowering periods extend over the middle of the summer. *L. washingtonianum* is a stoloniferous species with no stem-roots. The seed has delayed hypogeal germination. This lily seems to like a deep loamy soil, preferably acid or neutral. There are a couple of varieties, namely var. *minor*, known as the shasta lily, which has white flowers and is smaller than the hue species, and var. *purpurascens*, which ages to a deeper colour than the true species. The latter is the form most commonly seen in gardens.

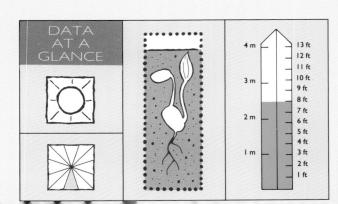

L. wigginsii
~

This Turk's-cap lily from the western side of the United States is a rich yellow dotted with purple spots. It flowers about mid summer and grows to 4 ft (1.20 m) tall. It is a rhizomatous bulb with occasional stem roots. The seed has delayed hypogeal germination. Grow in an acid, moisture-retentive soil.

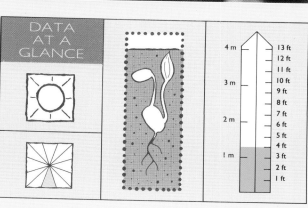

DATA
AT A
GLANCE

Cardiocrinum giganteum

Cardiocrinum giganteum
~

Although it now belongs to a different genus, this bulbous plant from the Himalayas is still regarded as a lily by most growers and definitely has a place in this book. Its former name was *Lilium giganteum*, and gigantic it is, growing up to 12 ft (3.60 m) high when conditions suit it. These tall stems carry up to 25 trumpet-shaped flowers that face downwards, which is fortunate otherwise it would be impossible to see into them at that height. The individual flowers are also large, each being up to 8 in (20 cm) long. They are pure white in colour with reddish-purple markings in the throat. For those people tall enough, the flowers are fragrant. The species flowers from early to late summer. The germination is epigeal, but it is usually delayed, making growing cardiocrinums from seed a very long process. Seed should be sown every year so that after a few years' delay there will be a constant supply of flowering bulbs despite the long maturing process. Unfortunately, this species is monocarpic and the plants die after flowering, but small offsets are sometimes produced around the main bulb and these should be detached and grown on. The bulb needs shallow planting. In order to get large plants the soil should be adequately supplied with organic material and the plant itself lightly shaded. The seed capsules make wonderful dried decorations. While the type plant comes from the Himalayas there is a variety *yunnanense* that comes from China. It is very similar, the only obvious difference being that it is shorter.

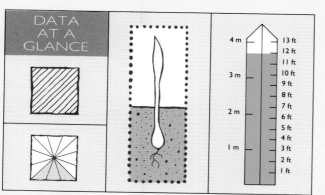

Cardiocrinum cordatum
~

Formerly known as *Lilium cordatum*, this is another similar species, this time coming mainly from Japan. It is shorter than *C. giganteum*, growing up to 6 ft (1.80 m) tall, but in most other respects, including flower colour, is similar to it. It, too, is monocarpic and needs replacing each year.

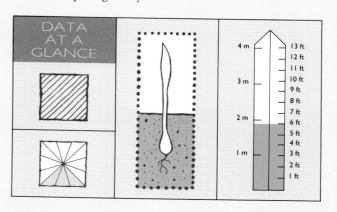

A–Z OF LILY HYBRIDS

Names given in single quotes are hybrids or cultivars, where all plants of that name should be identical. They can only be perpetuated by vegetative means. Those not given in quotes are strains, or grex, and consist of plants that can vary in some characteristics and are not necessarily identical in all details but originate from the same seed parents. These can be grown from seed.

Numbers given after the name refer to the division to which the lily belongs in the classification of cultivars.

LEFT This lily, 'Enchantment', flowers enthusiastically in early summer.
~

BELOW African Queen lilies can be produced in shades varying from creamy colour to apricot; they all have the advantage of being scented.
~

African Queen Strain

~

VI (a) This strain consists of a wonderful selection of scented trumpet lilies varying from warm yellow to apricot in colour. They are very floriforous with up to 12 flowers per stem, and flower from mid to late summer on stems which reach up to 6 ft (1.80 m) in height. They will grow on limy soils and will tolerate partial shade.

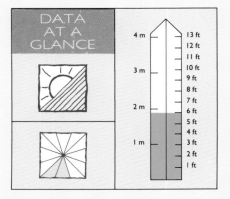

'Apeldoorn'

~

I (a) An upward-facing Asiatic hybrid with a star-shaped flower of bright orange briefly touched with dark purple spots. It is a strong-growing plant with up to a dozen flowers per stem. It flowers during mid summer and grows up to 3 ft (90 cm) in height. It will tolerate limy soils.

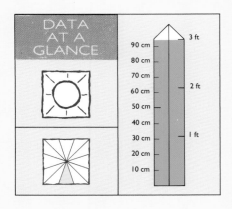

'Atilla'
~

I (b) This large-flowered Asiatic hybrid is outward-facing and has dark creamy-yellow petals speckled with dark brown spots. It is a strong-growing lily that reaches up to 3 ft (90 cm) in height. It flowers in mid summer and tolerates limy soils.

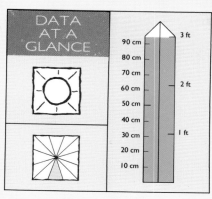

DATA AT A GLANCE

90 cm — 3 ft
80 cm
70 cm
60 cm — 2 ft
50 cm
40 cm
30 cm — 1 ft
20 cm
10 cm

Aurelian Hybrids
~

VI (a) These are a wonderful strain of trumpet lilies developed in the 1930s, in a wide range of colours from which many individual hybrids have been named. They flower in mid summer and grow up to 5 ft (1.50 m) tall. They should grow in limy soils if sufficient humus is added.

Backhouse Hybrids
~

II   A range of martagon hybrids from the end of the 19th century, of which some have been given individual names. The pendant flowers come in a wide selection of colours from yellow and cream to pinks and red. They bloom from early to mid summer and rise on stems up to 6 ft (1.80 m) high. There are no problems with limy conditions.

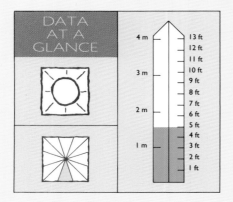

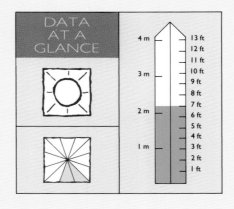

Bellingham Hybrids
~

IV An old strain of hybrids raised in America at the end of the
First World War. These are good tough lilies, more resistant to
virus than many other forms. They are quite floriferous, with up
to 20 pendant flowers which appear in early to mid summer in a
range of colours from yellow to bright orange-red with brown-
red spotting. The stems are up to 7 ft (2 m) tall. They are well
suited to a range of soils.

'Bingo'
~

I (b) This is one of the shortest of the Asiatic hybrids (12–18 in/
30–45 cm). Its outward-facing flowers are an orange-red, fading
towards the throat. They appear from early to mid summer and
the shortness of their stems makes them ideal for growing in
containers. They will tolerate a limy soil.

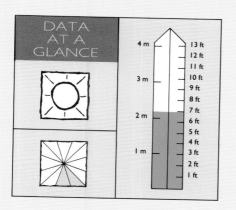

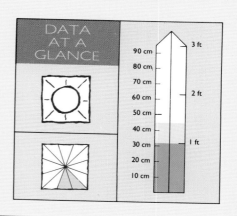

'Black Beauty'

~

VII (d) This is an Oriental hybrid with very reflexed petals. The flowers are a rich red with white edges to the petals and a green central 'star'. 'Black Beauty' is a very easy hybrid to grow, with masses of very fragrant flowers in mid summer, on stems 3–6 ft (90 cm–1.80 m) high. It is a stem-rooter so it should be planted deep. Avoid planting it on limy soils.

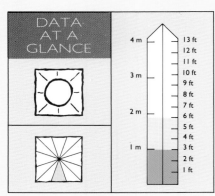

DATA AT A GLANCE

4 m — 13 ft / 12 ft / 11 ft
3 m — 10 ft / 9 ft / 8 ft
2 m — 7 ft / 6 ft / 5 ft / 4 ft
1 m — 3 ft / 2 ft / 1 ft

'Bonfire'
~

VII (b) A striking, large, bowl-shaped lily with deep crimson petals, strongest at the midrib and fading to a silvery white on the margins and reverse. It is also spotted in crimson. Flowering in late summer, it reaches up to 5 ft (1.50 m) in height. This cultivar does not like limy soils.

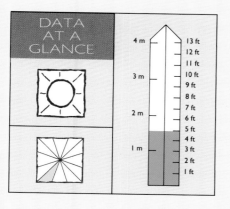

'Bright Star'
~

VI (d) The star here is the bright orange centre to the white flower. 'Bright Star' is one of the trumpet lilies, this time with quite a flat flower with recurved tips to the petals. It is easy to grow and produces about a dozen scented flowers on stems that reach 3–4 ft (90 cm–1.20 m) or more. The flowers appear in mid summer. This lily will grow on chalky or limy soils.

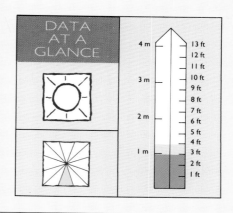

'Bull's Eye'
~

I (b) The flowers of this lily are bowl-shaped and outward-facing. They are striking in appearance, being bright lemon-yellow with a strong red eye. This lily flowers in early summer and will grow up to 3 ft (90 cm) tall. It should tolerate limy soils.

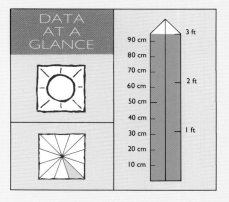

'Casablanca'
~

VII (b) A superb white Oriental hybrid with a hint of a green star in the centre against which the orange-brown anthers stand out in contrast. The flower-head is massive being up to 10 in (25 cm) in diameter, with the petals forming in a shallow bowl and recurved at their tips. Added to all this it is strongly scented. It is in flower from late summer into autumn. In height 'Casablanca' grows to about 3–4 ft (90 cm–1.20 m). It is a stem-rooter and will not grow on limy soils.

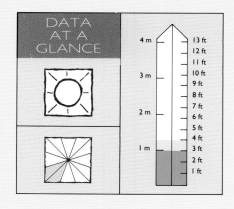

Citronella Strain

~

I (c) These are Asiatic hybrids of a pendant persuasion. Being a strain the colour varies, from a golden to a lemon yellow in this case, each speckled with black spots. This is a very vigorous, long-lasting and prolific strain, each flower stem bearing up to 30 flowers. Flowering takes place in mid summer on stems up to 5 ft (1.50 m) in height. Plants of this strain will tolerate lime.

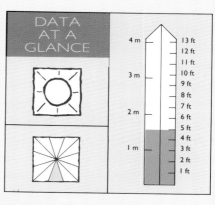

DATA AT A GLANCE

4 m — 13 ft / 12 ft / 11 ft

3 m — 10 ft / 9 ft / 8 ft

2 m — 7 ft / 6 ft / 5 ft

1 m — 4 ft / 3 ft / 2 ft / 1 ft

'Colleen'

~

I (a) A floriferous upward-facing lily with cream flowers that fade to white as they age. There are purple spots at the base of the petals, and the brown pollen adds to the contrast. It grows up to 3 ft (90 cm) in height, bearing flowers around mid summer. It is lime tolerant.

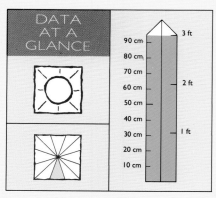

DATA AT A GLANCE

90 cm — 3 ft
80 cm
70 cm
60 cm — 2 ft
50 cm
40 cm
30 cm — 1 ft
20 cm
10 cm

'Connecticut Beauty'
~

I (a) This lily is also known as 'Médaillon' (or, incorrectly, as 'Medallion'). It has upward-facing flowers with soft yellow petal that darken towards the throat; they appear from early to mid summer and are borne on stems up to 3 ft (90 cm) in height. It should tolerate limy conditions.

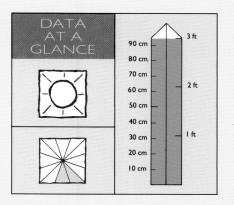

'Connecticut King'
~

I (a) This is an Asiatic hybrid of distinction, belonging to a long line of Connecticut Hybrids. The flowers are a rich golden yellow, slightly paling towards the tips of the petals. They have the twin advantages of being unspotted and upward-facing, making this lily a very popular one for cutting. Flowering takes place in mid summer, when growth will reach up to 3 ft (90 cm). This lily is vigorous and will tolerate lime.

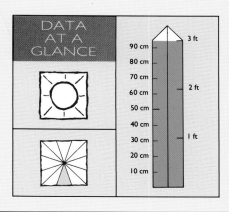

'Connecticut Lemonglow'
~

I (b) Outward-facing flowers of a refreshing pure, unspotted yellow. These appear about mid summer on stems that can reach up to 5 ft (1.50 m) high. This lily is sometimes seen named 'Gold Coast'. The plant is lime tolerant.

'Corina'
~

I (a) Another Asiatic hybrid with upward-facing flowers, this time coloured a fine red with a brown-dotted centre and reddish-brown anthers. It is in flower in the early summer and grows to about 3 ft (90 cm) in height. This hybrid will tolerate lime in the soil.

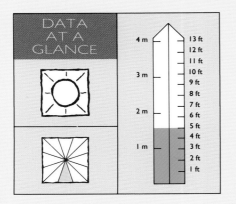

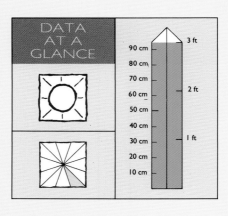

'Corsage'
~

I (b) A wonderful, long-lasting lily, particularly good for cutting, and it has the advantage of producing no pollen. It is an Asiatic hybrid with outward-facing flowers, the reflexed petal tips being a rose pink which fade to a creamy white towards the centre. This paler area is covered with maroon spots. Each stem contains up to 12 blooms and the plant flowers in mid summer on stems up to 4 ft (1.20 m) in height. It will tolerate limy conditions.

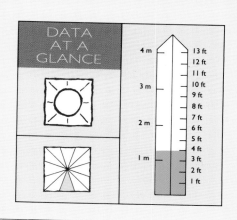

'Destiny'
~

I (a) This attractive lily has upward-facing flowers of a yellow coloration speckled with dark brown spots. The tips of the petals are reflexed. It flowers in early summer on stems that can reach up to 4 ft (1.20 m) high. It will grow on most soils, tolerating limy ones.

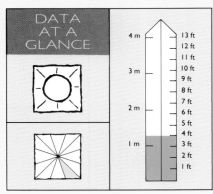

DATA AT A GLANCE

4 m — 13 ft
12 ft
11 ft
3 m — 10 ft
9 ft
8 ft
7 ft
2 m — 6 ft
5 ft
4 ft
1 m — 3 ft
2 ft
1 ft

'Edith'

~

I (a) A floriferous, upward-facing lily with pale yellow or cream petals, lightly spotted in black towards the pale green centre. The large flowers are borne in mid summer on stems up to 4 ft (1.20 m) high. It is lime tolerant.

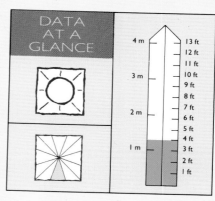

DATA AT A GLANCE

4 m — 13 ft
12 ft
11 ft
3 m — 10 ft
9 ft
8 ft
2 m — 7 ft
6 ft
5 ft
1 m — 4 ft
3 ft
2 ft
1 ft

'Enchantment'

~

I (a) This is a selected form from the famous Mid-Century Hybrids and has gone on to become one of the most popular of lilies. It is an upward-facing Asiatic hybrid having cup-shaped flowers of a vivid orange-red, with black spotting in their centres. It is a vigorous and prolific flowerer with up to 16 blooms per stem, making it an excellent cut flower for the early summer. It is also possible to force this lily to flower earlier. It grows up to 3 ft (90 cm) tall. It will tolerate limy soils.

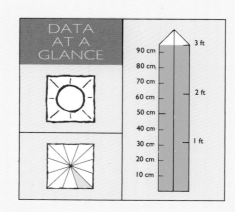

'Fire King'

~

I (b) This is a lily first made popular in the 1930s but still going strong. It is a very prolific Asiatic hybrid which is often absolutely covered (up to 20 flowers per stem) in funnel-shaped flowers with reflexed tips. The flowers are bright orange-red, each spotted with purple. This lily grows up to 3 ft (90 cm) high, and flowers during the mid-summer period. It will tolerate lime.

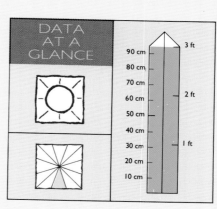

Golden Splendour Strain
~

VI (a) This is a very good strain of outward-facing trumpet lilies that appear in a range of yellows, each with a dark red stripe on the reverse of the petals. Lilies of this strain are strong-growing, vigorous and long-lasting. They flower in mid summer and grow up to 4 ft (1.20 m) tall. They will grow on limy soils.

Green Magic Strain
~

VI (a) A cool-coloured strain of trumpet-shaped lilies which are mainly white, but with varying degrees of green tinge, getting darker towards the middle. These lilies are very prolific with up to 20 flowers per stem. They flower in mid summer and will reach up to 6 ft (1.80 m) in height. They will grow on limy soils.

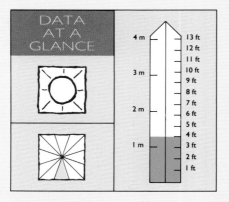

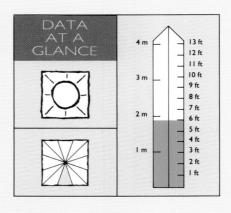

Harlequin Strain

~

I (c) Asiatic hybrids with pendant, Turk's-cap flowers that appear in a very wide range of colours encompassing virtually all lily colours; hence Harlequin is an apt name. The flowers are splashed with red or brown spots. Mid summer is their flowering time, and they will reach up to 5 ft (1.50 m) high. They make a very good hardy and vigorous strain that does well on most soils.

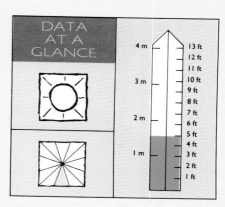

DATA AT A GLANCE

4 m — 13 ft
— 12 ft
— 11 ft
3 m — 10 ft
— 9 ft
— 8 ft
2 m — 7 ft
— 6 ft
— 5 ft
— 4 ft
1 m — 3 ft
— 2 ft
— 1 ft

'Imperial Crimson'

~

VII (c) This is a strain of fragrant, large-flowered lilies. The flowers are very flat and each petal has a white margin to its main coloration of rich crimson. They appear in the late summer. It is quite a tall lily, reaching up to 5 ft (1.50 m) in height. It prefers a rich soil but will tolerate lime.

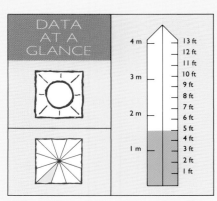

DATA AT A GLANCE

4 m   13 ft
   12 ft
   11 ft
3 m   10 ft
   9 ft
   8 ft
   7 ft
2 m   6 ft
   5 ft
   4 ft
1 m   3 ft
   2 ft
   1 ft

'Imperial Gold'

~

VII (c) A large-flowered (up to 10 in/25 cm in diameter), Oriental hybrid, ivory white in colour, with a golden stripe down the centre of each petal and maroon spotting. Up to 12 of these large, flat, wonderfully scented flowers grow on each stem. This lily grows up to 6 ft (1.80 m) tall, and does not appreciate being grown on chalk or limy soils.

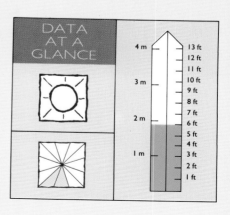

DATA
AT A
GLANCE

4 m — 13 ft
12 ft
11 ft
3 m — 10 ft
9 ft
8 ft
2 m — 7 ft
6 ft
5 ft
4 ft
1 m — 3 ft
2 ft
1 ft

'Imperial Silver'
~

VII (c) A similar lily to 'Imperial Gold'. The flower is a pure white, and lacks the gold stripe, but retains the maroon spots. It is equally large and vigorous and flowers at the same time.

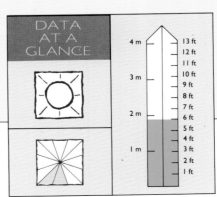

'Jetfire'

~

I (a) A superbly coloured Asiatic hybrid, whose upward-facing flowers are a deep orange fading to a rich yellow in the centre, with no spots to spoil the effect. It has up to 12 flowers per stem, and blooms from early to mid summer. It grows up to 3 ft (90 cm) tall and will tolerate chalk.

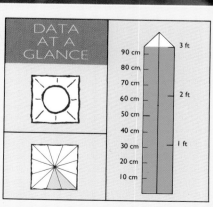

'Journey's End'
~

VII (d) A beautiful, Oriental hybrid with rich crimson-pink petals which fade to white at the edges and reflexed tips. The flowers are darker towards their middle and have yet darker spots. They have a good scent and bloom in late summer or early autumn. 'Journey's End' is a prolific flowerer with up to 15 blooms per stem and will grow up to 6 ft (1.80 m) high. It dislikes limy soils.

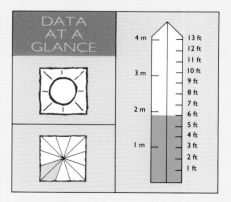

'Lady Ann'
~

VI (b)–(c) A lily in a lovely apricot-yellow colour, deeper in the throat and paler towards the tips of the petals. The brown pollen on the anthers stands out as a wonderful contrast. 'Lady Ann' is a strong grower with long-lasting flowers, which bloom in mid to late summer. The plant grows up to 5 ft (1.50 m). It will grow on limy soils.

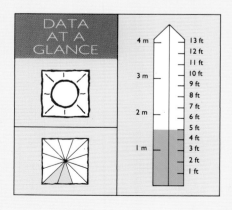

'Limelight'
~

VI (a) A popular trumpet lily with pale yellow flowers touched with green. It is mid-summer flowering and will grow in either sun or light shade. The stems can reach up to 6 ft (1.80 m). It will grow on limy soil.

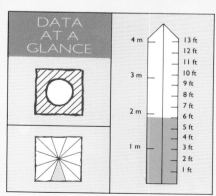

DATA AT A GLANCE

4 m — 13 ft
— 12 ft
— 11 ft
3 m — 10 ft
— 9 ft
— 8 ft
— 7 ft
2 m — 6 ft
— 5 ft
— 4 ft
1 m — 3 ft
— 2 ft
— 1 ft

'*Mabel Violet*'

~

VI (a) This trumpet lily is of a colour rarely seen in lilies: violet, or at least nearly violet. A dark pink with a green-pink throat would be a better description, but it is still unusual. This strong-growing lily flowers in mid summer and will reach up to 4 ft (1.20 m). It is possible to grow it on limy soils.

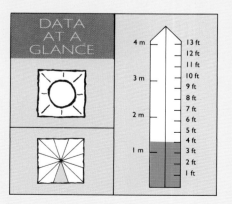

'*Marhan*'

~

II A very old *martagon-hansonii* hybrid from the end of the 19th century that is still going strong. The pendant, Turk's-cap flowers are orange, spotted with reddish brown. It blooms early in the summer and the stems can reach up to 6 ft (1.80 m). It presents no problems on limy soils.

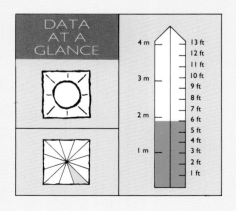

Mid-Century Hybrids
~

I (a) These are upward-facing Asiatic hybrids in bright colours from yellow through orange to red, first produced in 1949 as their name suggests. They have, in turn, provided many named hybrids. They flower in early summer and are relatively short, reaching up to 3 ft (90 cm) high. There should be no problem with most soils.

'Mont Blanc'
~

I (a) A white lily with upward-facing flowers. It is lightly spotted with fine dots towards the base of the petals. It comes into flower around mid summer on shortish stems that are up to 2 ft (60 cm) in height. It should be lime tolerant.

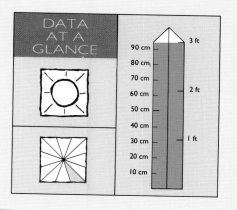

DATA AT A GLANCE

90 cm — 3 ft
80 cm
70 cm
60 cm — 2 ft
50 cm
40 cm
30 cm — 1 ft
20 cm
10 cm

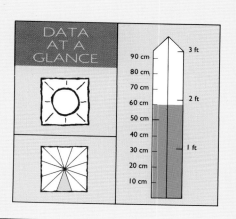

DATA AT A GLANCE

90 cm — 3 ft
80 cm
70 cm
60 cm — 2 ft
50 cm
40 cm
30 cm — 1 ft
20 cm
10 cm

'Montreux'

~

I (a) A lovely, pink-flowering, Asiatic hybrid, whose upward-facing, cup-shaped flower has a dusting of brown spots in the throat. It is a shortish lily growing up to 3 ft (90 cm) and it flowers in mid summer. It will tolerate limy soils.

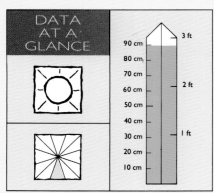

DATA AT A GLANCE

90 cm — 3 ft
80 cm
70 cm
60 cm — 2 ft
50 cm
40 cm
30 cm — 1 ft
20 cm
10 cm

Moonlight Strain

~

VI (a) A series of greenish yellow trumpet lilies, with the green particularly noticeable on the central vein. They are a strong-growing, hardy strain that flower in mid summer and reach up to 6 ft (1.80 m) in height.

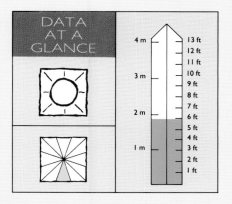

'Mrs R.O. Backhouse'

~

II A very prolific Turk's-cap lily that will, under favourable conditions, carry up to 30 flowers. These flowers are an orange-yellow, speckled with red spots, and the outside of the flowers is tinged with a magenta rose. This is one of the older plants, introduced in 1921 and named after the raiser. It flowers in early summer and will grow up to 6 ft (180 m) tall. This lily will grow on limy soils.

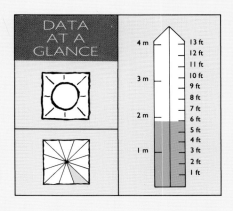

'Moulin Rouge'

~

I (b) An outward-facing Asiatic hybrid with rich orange-red flowers blotched and spotted with darker colours. It flowers in mid summer and grows to a height of up to 4 ft (1.20 m). It is lime tolerant.

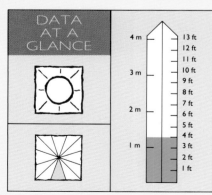

Olympic Hybrids
~

VI (a) A classic race of hybrid trumpet lilies produced soon after the Second World War, and varying in colour from white through cream to pink. They also include some lilies with cool green flowers. The throat of the flower is usually yellow and the flowers are fragrant. These lilies grow up to 6 ft (1.80 m) high and flower in mid summer. They will grow on limy soils.

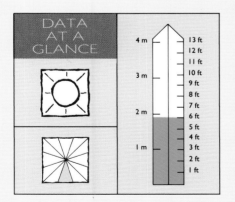

'Paisley Hybrids'
~

II A strain of Turk's-cap lilies in varying shades of yellow through to browns and purples, and touched with maroon spots. They flower in early summer and reach a height of 5 ft (1.50 m). They are both lime and shade tolerant.

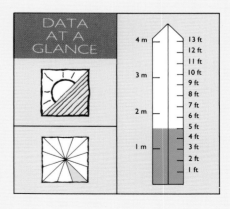

Pink Pearl Strain

~

VI (a) A strain of scented trumpet hybrids that are a rich purplish pink on the outside and a lighter pink on the inside. They flower from mid to late summer and can reach up to 5 ft (1.50 m) in height. Lilies of this strain can be grown on limy soils.

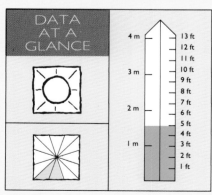

DATA AT A GLANCE

4 m — 13 ft
 — 12 ft
 — 11 ft
3 m — 10 ft
 — 9 ft
 — 8 ft
 — 7 ft
2 m — 6 ft
 — 5 ft
 — 4 ft
1 m — 3 ft
 — 2 ft
 — 1 ft

Pink Perfection Strain
~

VI (a) A very good strain of deep pink trumpet-shaped flowers. They are very prolific, producing up to 20 fragrant flowers per stem, which bloom in mid summer and can be up to 6 ft (1.80 m) tall. They will tolerate limy conditions.

'Red Band Hybrids'
~

VII (b) Outward-facing, bowl-shaped lilies with ruffled petals, which are white with broad bands varying from pink to crimson down the centre of each petal. They are also speckled in the same colours. The illustration shows 'Pink Ribbons'. These scented flowers appear in late summer and are up to 5 ft (1.50 m) tall. The plant will not grow on limy soils.

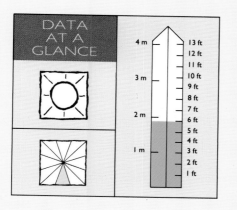

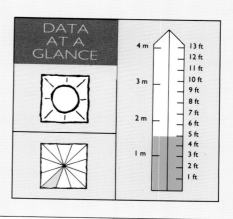

'Rosepoint Lace'
~

I (b) This outward-facing Asiatic hybrid is a new introduction from the United States. The star-shaped lily has creamy petals, heavily marked with rose, giving it a marbled effect. It is fragrant. 'Rosepoint Lace' is a vigorous and, so far, disease-resistant variety that flowers in early summer. It will grow up to 5 ft (1.50 m) tall. Unfortunately it dislikes limy soils.

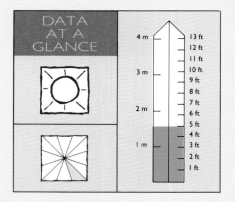

'Rosita'
~

I (a) An upward-facing Asiatic hybrid of an unusual colour, namely a purple-pink, stronger towards the central midrib. The cup-shaped flower also has a slight dark spotting. 'Rosita' is a vigorous lily with long-lasting flowers which make it an excellent flower for cutting. It is an early flowering lily and grows up to 3 ft (90 cm). It will tolerate limy soils.

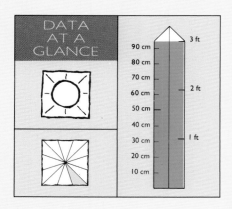

'Roter Cardinal'

~

I (a) This lily is also known as 'Red Night', both names acknow-
ledging the deep red colour of this very attractive upward-facing
lily. There are some darker red spots in the throat. It flowers
around mid summer and will grow up to 3 ft (90 cm) high. It
should be lime tolerant.

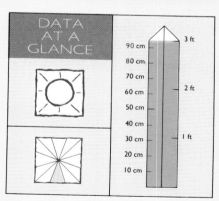

DATA
AT A
GLANCE

90 cm   3 ft
80 cm
70 cm
60 cm   2 ft
50 cm
40 cm
30 cm   1 ft
20 cm
10 cm

'Safari'
~

I (a) Upward-facing Asiatic hybrids. This lily has a vivid coloration with orange-red petals with black spots, and a yellow patch towards the base. The flowers open in mid summer and grow on stems that reach up to 4 ft (1.20 m) high. They should be lime tolerant.

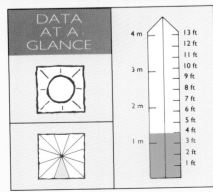

'Shuksan'

~

IV This Turk's-cap is one of the finest of the Bellingham Hybrids, with up to 16 nodding flowers per stem each a yellow-orange flushed with a touch of red and splashed with maroon spots. As well as being vigorous 'Shuksan' is very long-lasting, making it an ideal cut flower. It grows up to 6 ft (1.80 m) high and flowers in mid summer. It will tolerate limy soils.

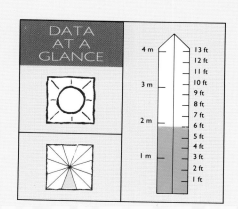

DATA AT A GLANCE

4 m — 13 ft
12 ft
11 ft
3 m — 10 ft
9 ft
8 ft
2 m — 7 ft
6 ft
5 ft
4 ft
1 m — 3 ft
2 ft
1 ft

'Star Gazer'

~

VII (c) This is one of the Oriental hybrids with upward-facing flowers. These flowers are quite flat with reflexed tips to the petals. They are a rich crimson, paling to white on the margins and spotted with a dark red. It is a fragrant lily that flowers in mid summer, although it is a good plant for forcing in pots to produce early flowers. It grows up to 5 ft (1.50 m). It will not grow on lime but will happily grow in pots or containers.

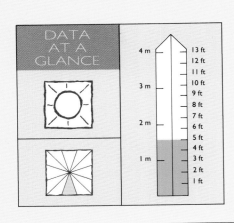

DATA AT A GLANCE

4 m — 13 ft
12 ft
11 ft
3 m — 10 ft
9 ft
8 ft
7 ft
2 m — 6 ft
5 ft
4 ft
1 m — 3 ft
2 ft
1 ft

'Sterling Star'

~

I (a) An upward-facing, cup-shaped lily with white petals, shaded

with cream and, to add contrast, brown spots and brown pollen.

The flowers appear from early to mid summer on stems of up to

4 ft (1.20 m). The plant is lime tolerant.

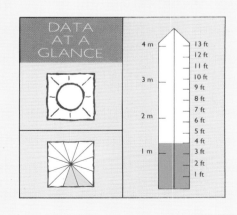

'Sun Ray'

~

I (a) An upward-facing Asiatic hybrid with lemon yellow flowers touched with a few brown spots. It is an early to mid-summer flowering lily and will grow up to 3 ft (90 cm) in height. It will tolerate limy conditions.

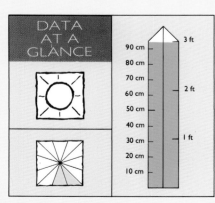

DATA
AT A
GLANCE

90 cm — 3 ft
80 cm
70 cm
60 cm — 2 ft
50 cm
40 cm
30 cm — 1 ft
20 cm
10 cm

'Sylvester'
~

I (a) An upward-facing Asiatic hybrid of a pure golden colour, touched with a light brown spotting. It flowers in early summer on shortish stems that are up to 2 ft (60 cm) high. It should be lime tolerant.

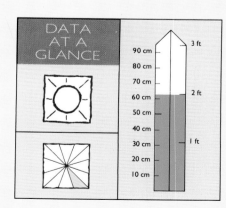

DATA AT A GLANCE

90 cm — 3 ft
80 cm
70 cm
60 cm — 2 ft
50 cm
40 cm
30 cm — 1 ft
20 cm
10 cm

'Tamara'
~

I (a) An upward-facing lily with a curious, but attractive, combination of colours varying from soft reddish colours at the tips of the petals to soft orange-yellow towards the throat and speckled with purple spots. It is a mid summer flowerer, reaching up to 3 ft (90 cm) in height. It should tolerate limy soils.

'Theseus'
~

(Ic) A downward-facing, sterile Asiatic hybrid with rich red Turk's-cap flowers. It is a vigorous plant that produces its wonderful scented flowers in mid summer. 'Theseus' grows up to 6 ft (1.80 m) high. It is not very happy in limy soils.

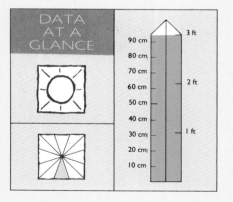

DATA AT A GLANCE

90 cm — 3 ft
80 cm
70 cm
60 cm — 2 ft
50 cm
40 cm
30 cm — 1 ft
20 cm
10 cm

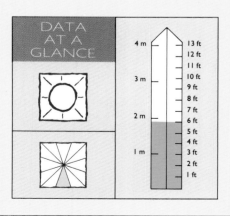

DATA AT A GLANCE

4 m — 13 ft
12 ft
11 ft
3 m — 10 ft
9 ft
8 ft
7 ft
2 m — 6 ft
5 ft
4 ft
1 m — 3 ft
2 ft
1 ft

'Venture'

~

I (a) An asiatic hybrid with upward-facing flowers with petals that are slightly recurved and of a wonderful strong red dotted with black spots. They appear from early into mid summer on stems that reach up to 5 ft (1.50 m). It should be lime tolerant.

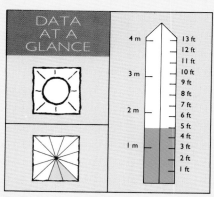

'Yellow Blaze'

~

I(a) An upward-facing Asiatic hybrid with cup-shaped yellow flowers, speckled with dark brown spots. It blooms from mid to late summer and grows up to 5 ft (1.50 m) high. It should grow on limy soils if given plenty of humus.

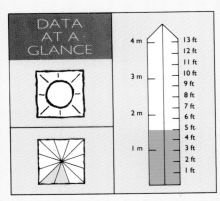

DATA AT A GLANCE

4 m — 13 ft
— 12 ft
— 11 ft
3 m — 10 ft
— 9 ft
— 8 ft
— 7 ft
2 m — 6 ft
— 5 ft
— 4 ft
1 m — 3 ft
— 2 ft
— 1 ft

'Zephyr'

~

I (a) A very floriferous lily with up to 25 blooms per stem. It is a cup-shaped, upward-facing Asiatic hybrid with soft pink flowers, flecked with tiny black spots and touched with a darker pink on the outside of the petals. It flowers in the early summer on stems up to 5 ft (1.50 m) tall. It will tolerate suitably fed limy soils.

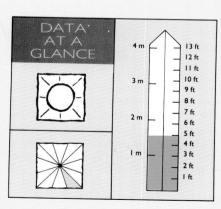

DATA AT A GLANCE

4 m — 13 ft
12 ft
11 ft
3 m — 10 ft
9 ft
8 ft
7 ft
2 m — 6 ft
5 ft
4 ft
1 m — 3 ft
2 ft
1 ft

GLOSSARY

acid soils Soils that have a pH lower than 7 (neutral). These will include peaty soils.

alkaline soils Soils with a pH greater than 7 (neutral). These will include chalky and limy soils.

anther The pad at the end of the stamen that contains the pollen. In the case of lilies they are versatile, ie they move about their mid point.

axil see *leaf axil.*

basal plate The solid plate at the bottom of the lily bulb to which the scales are attached and from which the roots descend.

bulbils Small bulbs that are formed above ground in the axils of the leaves.

bulblets Small bulbs that are formed below ground either as offsets to the main bulb or from the part of the stem that is below ground.

calcifuge A plant that dislikes an alkaline soil.

capsule The vessel that contains the mature seeds. In the lily the capsules are of varying shapes.

clone All plants that have been reproduced vegetatively from the parent plant, and have the same genetic make-up and hence appearance.

compost A mixture composed of rotted organic garden waste used for enriching or mulching the soil.

cotyledon The seed leaf, which is always the first to appear above ground. In most plants the cotyledon(s) are not the same shape as the true leaves which subsequently appear on the stems.

cultivar A plant that is a variation (by colour, size, shape etc) of the true species which has arisen in cultivation. Cultivars are normally given distinct names which appear in inverted commas, eg 'Black Beauty'.

epigeal germination Germination in which the seed leaf (cotyledon) appears above ground.

filament The stem-like part of the stamen that carries the anther.

genus (plural *genera*) A collection of species that have certain characteristics in common. In this book two genera are described, namely *Lilium* and *Cardiocrinum*.

grex see *strain.*

humus Rotted organic matter, such as rotted leaves, farmyard manure, garden compost, peat etc.

hybrid A plant that is the result of cross-pollination of two species, either in the wild or in cultivation.

hypogeal germination Germination in which the seed leaf (cotyledon) remains below ground.

inflorescence The total number of flowers comprising the flower-head.

leaf axil The upper angle formed by the junction of the leaf (or its stalk) with the stem.

monocarpic Said of those plants that die after flowering and seeding. *Cardiocrinum* are monocarpic.

mulch A layer of organic matter, such as bark, rotted leaves, peat, farmyard manure etc, that is applied to the surface of the soil to suppress weeds, conserve moisture and protect from weather extremes.

nectaries Organs which produce nectar.

nectary furrow A groove at the base of the perianth segments in which the nectaries are found.

ovary The organ at the base of the style in which the seeds develop once the ovule has been fertilized.

ovule The 'egg' that is fertilized to produce the seed.

pedicel A flower stalk.

perianth segments The parts of the flower that would commonly be called petals, except in the case of lilies they comprise both the identical-looking petals and sepals.

pH A scale of hydrogen ion concentration indicating relative acid and alkaline values. Soil with a pH of 4.5 is extremely acid, 7 is neutral and 9.1 extremely alkaline.

recurved Reflexed or bent back. Many petals are recurved at their tips.

reverse The backs or outside of petals.

rhizome An underground stem that produces both roots and above-ground shoots.

segments see *perianth segments.*

species The individual units that make up a genus, thus *Lilium regale* is a species which is part of the genus *Lilium*. Species are always printed in *italic* type.

stamen The male part of a flower consisting of the filament and the pollen-bearing anther.

stigma The tip of the female part of the flower which is receptive to the pollen.

stolon An underground stem which produces a new bulb at its tip.

strain A range of hybrids that have come from the same parents but are not necessarily identical in every aspect; they often vary in colour for example. The name of a strain is not included in quotation marks, eg Citronella Strain. Grex has the same meaning.

style The stalk that connects the ovary and the stigma.

subspecies The classification unit below that of species.

variety A unit below either that of a species or subspecies that shows minor differences from either of these. Varieties often have horticultural significance rather than botanical importance.

vegetative reproduction Methods of reproducing plants using the vegetative parts of the plant, ie scales, bulbils, offsets, etc, rather than seed. Vegetative reproduction ensures offspring that are identical to the parent.

Lilium Corsage

INDEX

PICTURE CREDITS

The publishers would like to thank the following for supplying the illustrations for this book:

Courtesy of B & D Lilies: pages 15, 46 right, 56 left, 60 right, 72 right, 99, 102, 114, 116 and 122.

Broadleigh Gardens: pages 63, 69 left, 79, 80 left and 95.

Duncan Coombs: pages 84, 104 right and 120 right.

Danny McBride: artwork on page 12.

Steve Menges: page 96 left.

Gene Mirro: pages 13 bottom, 45, 47, 51, 52 left, 53 left, 55, 60 left, 64 right, 66, 67 right, 70 right, 71 bottom, 74, 101 and 111 right.

Netherlands Flowerbulb Information Centre: 82 left, 85 right and 110.

North American Lily Society: pages 54 left and 85 left.

Oregon Bulb Farms: pages 6, 9 top, 11 top, 28, 29, 42, 43, 83 left, 97 and 125.

Harry Smith Horticultural Photographic Collection: Jacket pictures, pages 32, 62 right, 67 left, 70 left, 91, 96 right, 100, 103, 104 left, 107 left, 109 left and 115.

J. Walkers Bulbs: pages 80 right and 81.

Cathy Wilkinson Barash: pages 4 and·5, 7, 8, 9 bottom, 10, 11 bottom, 13 top, 14, 16, 17, 18, 19, 20, 21, 22, 23, 24, 25, 26, 27, 30, 31, 33, 34, 35, 36, 38, 39, 40, 41, 44, 46 left, 48, 49, 50, 52 right, 53 right, 54 right, 56 right, 57, 58, 59, 61, 62 left, 64 left, 65, 68, 69 right, 71 top, 72 left, 73, 75, 76, 77, 78, 82 right, 83 right, 86, 87, 88, 89, 90, 92, 93, 94, 98, 105, 106, 107 right, 108, 109 right, 111 left, 112, 113, 117, 118, 119, 120 left, 121 and 123.